Patterns for Pregnancy

To my children

Patterns for Pregnancy

Belinda Musgrave

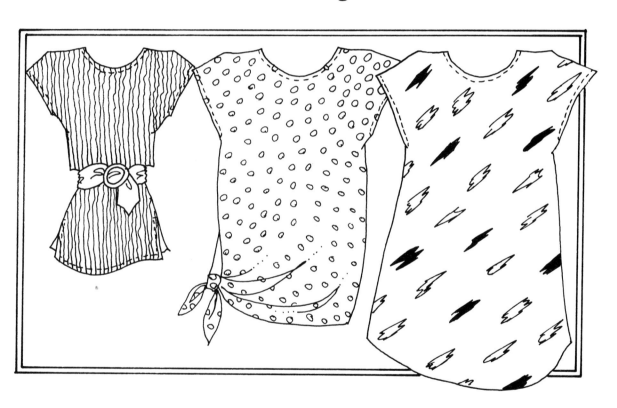

B.T. Batsford Ltd   London

Contents

© Belinda Musgrave 1987
First published 1987

ISBN 0 7134 5412 1

Printed in Great Britain by
Anchor Brendon Ltd
Tiptree, Essex
for the publishers B.T. Batsford Ltd
4 Fitzhardinge Street, London W1H 0AH

Acknowledgements

The author wishes to thank Joseph Yogerst for the photographs, and also Julia Clerk, William Musgrave and Jane Savvas for being models.

Introduction

Being pregnant is a very special nine months of a woman's life, when she is getting ready for the arrival of her baby. Her body shape changes drastically, so after the third month it is necessary to think about additional clothes which look attractive, feel comfortable and are not too tight over the bump. Women are often self-conscious about putting on the necessary weight, so it is extremely important to keep morale as high as possible by wearing attractive and flattering outfits.

After a quick look around the shops, you will soon realise that you must either pay a king's ransom for maternity clothes or patronise the very cheap end of the market and find yourself wearing identical outfits to every other mother-to-be. The best solution is to make a few outfits yourself. You can have fun selecting attractive fabrics and buying small, expensive trims and then sewing them together at a leisurely pace and at a fraction of the cost.

Patterns for Pregnancy is especially geared to women who have some experience of home dressmaking, no matter how limited, and therefore have commercial patterns which they have used before and like. The book illustrates several very simple methods of altering these patterns, of whatever size, into maternity shapes. By adapting everyday patterns, you can use styles which are right up-to-date, and need not be restricted to the traditional maternity patterns, and you can use them again, time after time, following the baby's arrival.

An introductory chapter on the importance of the design of maternity clothes is followed by tips on cutting out various fabrics, different methods of sewing the garments together and a chapter on individual decorative touches such as embroidery, appliqué, tucking and frills.

1. Design

Over the past few years there has been a complete revolution on the maternity wear scene. Mothers-to-be used to wear dull, dowdy colours in quite boring basic styles. It was regarded as a period of life which had to be endured, certainly not enjoyed. These days women's attitudes have changed; they have swapped their dowdy colours for vibrant hues and their basic styles for an exciting range of fashionable designs. It is a period of a woman's life when her skin glows, her hair shines and she looks beautiful, so it is only fitting that she should have attractive outfits which she enjoys wearing and feels comfortable in.

There are several advantages to making your own maternity clothes, the most important probably being the cost. For less than the price of a cheap outfit, you can design and make yourself a unique outfit using your own choice of fabrics and an expensive selection of trimmings. Never again will you be in the embarrassing situation of sitting in an ante-natal clinic wearing the identical dress to three or four other mothers-to-be. Cheap, off-the-peg outfits tend to be skimpy to keep within budget and they often become tight, uncomfortable and unsightly over the last few weeks. By making your own you will be able to include very fashionable style details, you can afford much more decorative detail and also ensure a perfect fit. A bit of gentle dressmaking can also be fun at this time when you certainly don't feel like embarking on energetic projects.

FIGURE TYPES

Are you tall and thin or short and plump? Have you got narrow shoulders or quite a large bust? The basic characteristics of your figure do not alter with pregnancy so you should stick to the rudimentary rules of styling for individual figure types and transfer them to maternity styles.

A very tall woman must select clothes which do not emphasise or exaggerate her height. For example, as vertical stripes tend to have this effect it would be wise to avoid them and perhaps replace them with more flattering diagonal stripes. Contrasting coloured separates, on the other hand, are ideal as they visually divide the body and so break up this illusion of height. A woman with this figure type would look most attractive in separates such as skirts and trousers with contrasting smocks or sweatshirts, slim skirts and blouson tops with hip sashes, or perhaps a dress which is made in a tiered style or one which is gathered in with a drawstring below the bump.

A shorter woman should do just the opposite. She must work hard to create and emphasise a vertical illusion of height, so blouson tops and contrasting sweatshirts would not really be flattering. Separates can be worn very successfully but they should be made of the same fabric or at least of fabrics of the same colour. All-in-one garments such as pinafores, dungarees and jumpsuits are ideal, and when dresses are selected they would be most flattering with vertical tucking or pleats. Do remember always to keep styling and accessories sleek, dainty and uncluttered.

◁ *1 Contrasting separates for a tall woman, and a printed dress with vertical tucking for a short woman*

Necklines and sleeves are important areas to emphasise in maternity wear as necks and arms always remain 'slim' areas. A woman with a long, graceful neck should accentuate it by wearing large pussy-cat bows, high Edwardian-type collars, upturned shirt collars or frilly necklines. On the other hand, a shorter neck calls for simpler necklines and open-neck styling. Sailor collars are perfect, as are rever styles or shirt and mandarin collars left unbuttoned at the top. Frilly collars may be worn but must be kept dainty. Sleeves should be carefully considered as very large ones will tend to broaden a woman's silhouette, and that's the last thing she will want. Full sleeves may be worn and are indeed flattering, especially for a woman with slightly heavy upper arms, but they will be most successful if worn short or at ¾-length so some of the arm is exposed. For long sleeves, either keep them slim fitting or gather the sleeve heads with the rest fitted on the principles of a leg-o-mutton style.

2 A high neckline flattering for a long neck, and a low neckline suitable for a short neck
▽

Sloping or narrow shoulders can easily be helped by tacking in a pair of shoulder pads; even a small pair makes a tremendous difference. Very broad shoulders, however, should be covered simply with the minimum of tucks, gathers or padding, as these will merely accentuate them.

3 Simple smock with leg-o-mutton type sleeves
▽

5 Lots of gathers and a lace frou-frou for a small ▷
bustline

A large bust is best disguised by keeping styling as sleek and plain as possible over this area. Do not wear dresses or tops with lots of gathering from shoulder yokes; instead select outfits with long bodice tucks or high waisted styles, both of which release the necessary fullness only over the bump. Plain outfits with attractive contrasting collars are very successful as they draw the eye upwards to the face. Bodices with frills, rows of braid, fancy buttons and appliquéd yokes, which would be totally wrong over a large bust, are, on the other hand, ideal for a flat-chested mother-to-be.

4 Smock with a very low yokeline suitable for a ▷
large bust

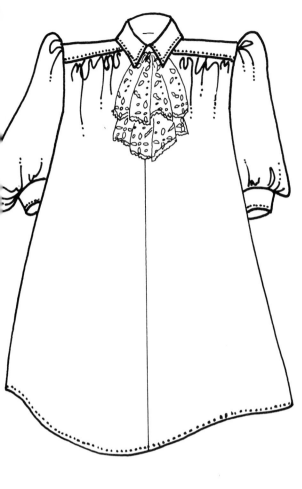

The woman who constantly updates her wardrobe to keep up with every new trend will find this book especially useful as she will have awful problems buying fashionable maternity clothes. She will be able to buy fabrics and trimmings which are bang up-to-date and make herself outfits imitating the very latest boutique ideas.

Very romantic women also seem to let their personalities dictate when selecting clothes. Without thinking they always seem to choose pastel colours, pretty fabrics, demure or romantic styles, frills, pin-tucks and feminine trims.

COLOUR AND FABRICS

The choice of colour, as discussed above, is a direct reflection of your personality; having selected a certain colour, you find that it plays a vital role in affecting your mood.

On a brilliant sunny day you automatically feel like wearing a bright outfit; a dull brown suit would be quite wrong. On a dreary wet cold day a grey dress can make you feel as cold and miserable as the weather itself, but if you must wear this dress do remember to cheer it up with a bright cardigan or a colourful scarf or some shiny costume jewellery. During winter months, dark colours are usually worn as these are warmer colours, but, as with the dreary grey dress, do add colourful blouses and jerseys, hats, scarves, jewellery and tights as these will cheer up both your outfit and you.

Dull-surfaced fabrics are more suited to maternity outfits, as they absorb light, giving a slimmer effect. Shiny fabrics, on the other hand, which reflect light and emphasise curves would be perfect for blouses and shirts worn under dungarees or pinafores as they would draw the eye away from the tummy.

It is advisable to choose washable fabrics for maternity outfits; as they are worn for such a short period it would be a shame to have them constantly at a dry-cleaners. Also, do not select very heavyweight fabrics, even for winter pregnancies, as you will probably find these far too hot to wear as most women seem to have inbuilt warmth over these months.

PERSONALITY

A flamboyant, outgoing woman can really go to town when selecting maternity outfits. She will want brilliant colours and dramatic styles because these express her personality and they are what she is used to wearing. Lots of gathering, masses of tucks, large sleeves, swirly printed fabrics, dramatic eye-catching collars, and then glittering fabrics and chunky jewellery for the evening. It is important not to try to change one's basic style of dress during these months and to feel as comfortable, normal and relaxed as possible. A flamboyant woman would, therefore, look as ridiculous as she would feel in a soft pink, pin spot dress with a neat Peter Pan collar. She may even find that she already owns outfits such as a flowing djellabah or a kaftan which she enjoys wearing and will easily cover her bump.

6   *The same dungaree pattern made in a cotton print for summer and in corduroy for winter*

SEASONS

A nine-month pregnancy will span three or four seasons, so it is important to select your wardrobe with the relevant seasons in mind. During the first three months most women continue to wear their everyday clothes, perhaps releasing a tight button or two around the waist. New clothes will be necessary for the fourth month as you will begin to look pregnant and not want to wear clothes which are at all restricting around the waistline. If your fourth month falls in the spring, you will want a spring and summer wardrobe with lots of lightweight fabrics in bright colours and summery styles. An autumn and winter pregnancy would suggest deeper, warmer colours and use of heavier fabrics such as brushed cotton, needlecord, denim or medium-weight jersey fabrics.

If your pregnancy spans winter and spring or summer and autumn your wardrobe will be more difficult to organise as you could have extremes of climate. Separates would be very useful garments as would pinafores and dungarees because, depending on the weather, you could add blouses or jerseys, a waistcoat, a cardigan or even a casual, unstructured jacket to suit your temperature.

In the following chapter a varied range of garments have been included which are suitable to span all seasons of the year. Obviously, several of the garments, such as the basic trousers, could be used for any season depending on the selected fabric. Cotton drill would make a lovely pair of summer trousers while the same pattern made in needlecord or gaberdine would suit the cooler seasons.

LIFESTYLE

Having considered basic figure types, personality, colour and seasons, it is next vital to think about your lifestyle whilst planning a maternity wardrobe. It would be silly to get carried away selecting outfits which are totally irrelevant to your life. If you are a working mother-to-be, you should obviously include a few smart outfits. A plain, dark-coloured pinafore and perhaps a pair of tailored pin-striped dungarees could be useful basic outfits. You could chop and change their appearance with tailored shirts or frilly blouses, bow ties or bright scarves, polo-necks or T-shirts

and still look very smart and efficient. A working mother-to-be will obviously need a few casual outfits for weekends and for when she stops working, but not as many as a woman who is expecting her second or third baby and who is at home far more of the time. This mother-to-be will need a casual, comfortable, more practical set of clothes such as a pair of jeans or trousers, a basic pinafore, a wrap-around skirt and a selection of complementary tops, T-shirts or jerseys. All the garments should be easily machine-washable as this expectant mother will be constantly hugged, cuddled and touched by her other toddlers with muddy boots and sticky jam-covered fingers. She must also have some special outfits for entertaining, dining out and parties.

The mother-to-be with a hectic, evening social life need not spend a fortune on her clothes. She could make herself a very plain, basic, black dress then use all the old tricks such as adding large detachable collars or yokes, colourful draped shawls, rows of wide ribbon, decorative buttons or even adding a shiny open jacket, to create the illusion of several outfits with hardly any expense.

GENERAL HINTS

Do remember when designing maternity clothes to make sure that you keep the necessary extra fullness exactly where you need it – over the bump! Emphasise all your slim areas such as arms, legs, neck and shoulders, as these help create a slimmer illusion. Do not make dresses with yards of flowing gathers from front yokes, back yokes and sleeve heads as you may end up looking like a ship in full sail.

If you usually wear very high heeled shoes and boots with rather long hemlines, do remember that mothers-to-be should wear flatter heels and therefore need shorter hemlines. To ensure a level maternity hemline the front should be dipped approximately 5-7.5cm (2-3in) lower than the back.

Remember to plan your hospital stay. Hospitals are always exceedingly hot places so it is nice to have two or three cool cotton nighties and a summerweight dressing-gown, even if it is in the depths of winter. If you are making simple cotton nighties, do include a long front opening as this is useful for breast-feeding.

2. Pattern Making

When beginning to organise a wardrobe for pregnancy it is often difficult to know where to start. If you begin by making one very basic item, like a simple top, you will then want a skirt or pair of co-ordinating trousers (or perhaps both) to go with it. These will spark off other ideas and, before you know it, you will have a lovely range of garments.

During pregnancy it is not only the tummy that grows – the whole body fills out slightly and so clothes need to be a size larger than usual. Ready-made maternity clothes and maternity patterns have taken this into account and the extra fullness has been included, but in order to make your own patterns for pregnancy these extra amounts must be added to your everyday commercial patterns. On average, the basic alterations are as follows.

increase bust circumference by 5cm (2in)
increase waist by 20-30cm (8-12in)
front hemline dipped by 5-7.5cm (2-3in)

To increase the bust measurement, 13mm (½in) is added parallel to front and back side seams. The same amount must also be added to the underarm seam of sleeves to make them correspond with the enlarged bodice.

The waistline will expand on average 20-30cm (8-12in), so this must be added to the pattern with most of this fullness over the tummy.

As your bump protrudes it will lift the front hemline, so this must be lengthened by about 5-7.5cm (2-3in) to make it appear level. This extra length will not really be necessary before the fifth or sixth month, so it is a good idea to incorporate it in the hem to begin with. When the extra length is needed it is a simple adjustment to let down the front hem. Cheap, off-the-peg garments often have straight hemlines which curve upwards and look dreadful in advanced pregnancy, so when making your own clothes it is well worth the extra trouble of dipping the hemline.

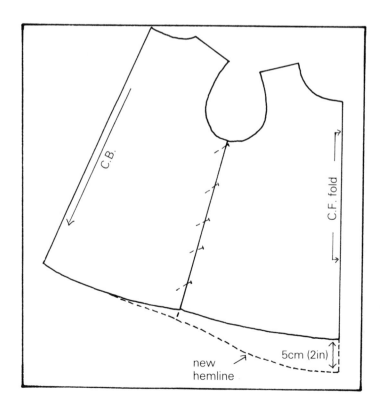

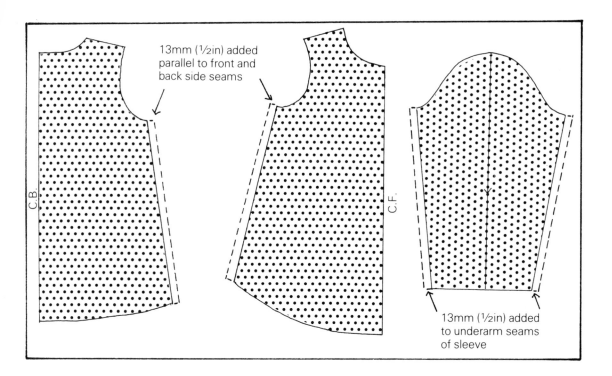

13mm (½in) added parallel to front and back side seams

13mm (½in) added to underarm seams of sleeve

C.B.

C.F.

△
7   13mm (¹/₂in) added to the pattern to make it a size larger

◁ 8   C.F. extended by 5cm (2in) to allow for the protrusion of the tummy

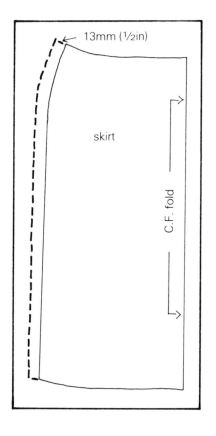

13mm (½in)

skirt

C.F. fold

Skirt patterns are made a size larger by adding 13mm (¹/₂in) parallel to the back and front side seams before beginning to adjust the waistline which is raised to sit comfortably above the tummy.

9   13mm (¹/₂in) added parallel to sides of skirt to ▷ make the pattern a size larger.

Trouser patterns are also made a size larger; 13mm (½in) is added parallel to front and back side seams from the waist to thigh level, then gradually tapered in to the original hemline to give a smooth side seam. The waistline is then raised to sit above the tummy.

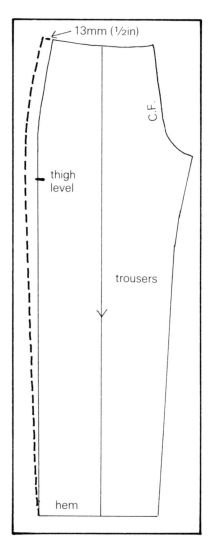

10   *13mm (½in) added to trousers from waist to thigh level then tapered to hem to make pattern a size larger*

The styles illustrated in this chapter have been selected from commercial pattern books to show the different methods of altering everyday commercial patterns into maternity shapes by adding fullness exactly where it is needed. Each pattern book has an endless number of blouse styles to choose from. They all look different, but the differences are principally because of the variety of collars, cuffs, pockets, sleeve lengths, etc. being used. If you ignore the collars, cuffs, pockets, sleeve lengths, etc. and look only at the body shape, you will find there are only a small variety of these body shapes. In fact, in each section of a typical pattern book, there are probably only three or four basic body shapes.

This chapter shows you how to adapt *only* the basic body shape of a commercial pattern into a maternity shape, because, after all, it is only the shape of the body which changes during pregnancy. Your arms and wrists and neck do not significantly change and so there is no need to alter the sleeves, cuffs and collars; these parts of the commercial pattern can be used in their original form with your new body shape.

Many of these patterns can be easily altered to suit cold or warm seasons, merely depending on the fabric selected; for example, the trousers could be made either in burgundy corduroy for winter and worn with a jersey, or in buttercup yellow poplin and worn with a stripy T-shirt for summer. The skirts could be made in fabrics of different weights depending on the season, as could the nighties and several of the tops and dresses.

ABBREVIATIONS USED

C.F.	centre front
C.B.	centre back
R.S.	right side
W.S.	wrong side
S.A.	seam allowance
R.S.U.	right side upwards (often used when the left and right sides of the pattern are different and therefore must be made individually).

For all patterns, metric and imperial measurements are given. Follow *either* set, but not a mixture of both, because they are not interchangeable.

Take note of all the markings on your commercial patterns, such as grain lines, balance marks or notches, foldlines, button positions, darts and areas of ease, etc. Always transfer them to your new pattern and add all new markings boldly. With all the necessary information clearly marked on your new pattern, the pieces will be recognisable at a glance and therefore be easy to place on fabric and cut out.

EQUIPMENT FOR MAKING MATERNITY PATTERNS

When making a pattern, several basic tools are needed, most of which you will already own.

> Several large sheets of papers – brown wrapping paper or large sheets of newsprint which can be purchased quite cheaply at art and craft shops. If neither of these are available, sheets of newspaper could be used.
>
> A pair of paper scissors.
>
> A pencil and rubber.
>
> A tape measure and a long ruler, both with metric and imperial measurements.
>
> A roll of sticky tape.
>
> A tracing wheel.
>
> A box of pins.
>
> A large flat surface to work on, either a large table or a large sheet of chipboard which can be placed over a small table or a couple of chairs and is easily stored under a bed.

MAKING THE PATTERN

Do not alter your commercial pattern. This must be kept intact so that you can easily refer back to it and also use it again after your pregnancy. Trace around the relevant pattern pieces onto large sheets of paper and transfer the pattern markings. Use this new, traced pattern for the alterations.

Keep your tape measure handy at all times. All the measurements given in this chapter are average measurements, so if you are extremely tall you will want to add extra length, whilst if you are quite petite you will want to shorten the patterns to keep in proportion.

Unless you have had a previous pregnancy you will not fully appreciate how much the body grows at this time, so do not skimp on the amount let into the width of the patterns – you will probably need it!

STYLE A

This is a very basic summer T-shirt which can be worn loose over trousers, shorts or a skirt, or can be given a slit at one side and knotted to give a draped effect.

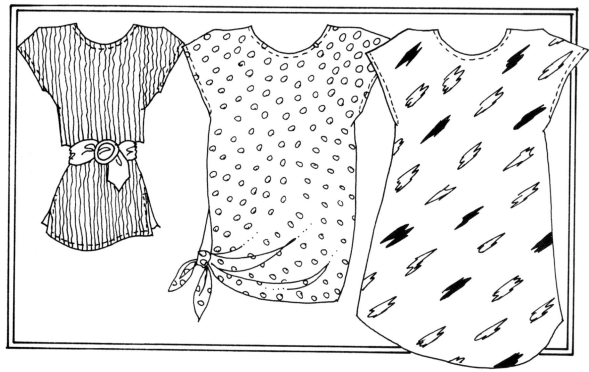

11 Style A: the original T-shirt and two maternity tops

12 Alteration to pattern A ▷

1 Trace around the front and back patterns and transfer the waist position and other markings.

2 Add 13mm (½) parallel to front and back side seams to make the pattern a size larger.

3 Hold the front pattern against yourself, and, looking in a mirror, mark the mid-point of your shoulder on the shoulder seam, and your bust point.

4 On the front pattern, draw a line from the mid-shoulder point (point A) through the bust point (B) down to the mid-point of the hem between C.F. and the side seam (point C).

5 Cut the pattern from point A through point B to point C.

6 Place both sections of front patterns on another sheet of paper.

7 Spread the shoulderline apart 2.5cm (1in) at point A.

8 At the waistline, which will be marked on your pattern, spread the pattern apart 7.5cm (3in) and secure the pattern to the paper beneath it.

9 Place the shoulders of the front and back patterns together and transfer point A to the shoulderline of the back pattern.

10 Draw a line from point A down to the mid-point of the back hem (point D). Cut the pattern along this line.

11 Place both back sections on another sheet of paper.

12 Spread the back shoulder 2.5cm (1in) apart at point A.

13 Spread the pattern 5cm (2in) apart at the waistline and secure the pattern to the sheet of paper beneath it.

You will now have increased the waist circumference by 25cm (10in). This should be enough for an average increase in waist circumference, but if a very loose fit is required the pattern could be spread apart even more at the waistline.

18

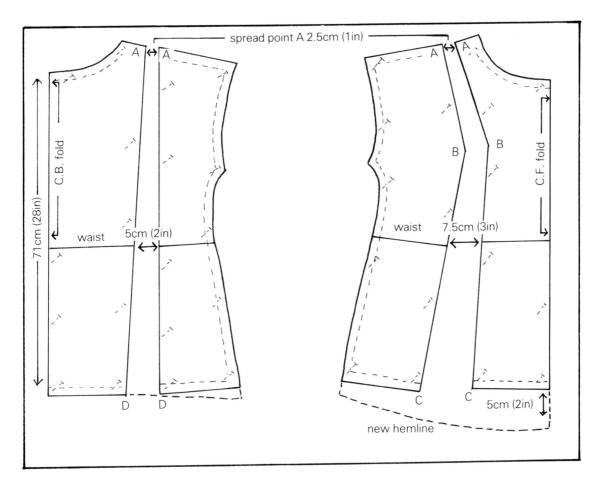

14 Pin front and back patterns together along the side seams to make a new hemline.

15 Decide on a finished C.B. length; an average length is 71cm (28in).

16 Increase the length of the front and back patterns equally then add another 5cm (2in) at C.F. to allow for the protrusion of the bump.

17 Join the C.F. to the C.B. with a smoothly curved hemline and add an extra allowance for the hem.

18 Separate front and back patterns.

19 If you wish to knot your T-shirt at the side, leave one side seam open 20cm (8in) when sewing your T-shirt, and carefully neaten the seam allowance.

The neck facings of this T-shirt are used in their original form as there has been no alteration to the neckline.

- - - - - - - - - - - - - - -

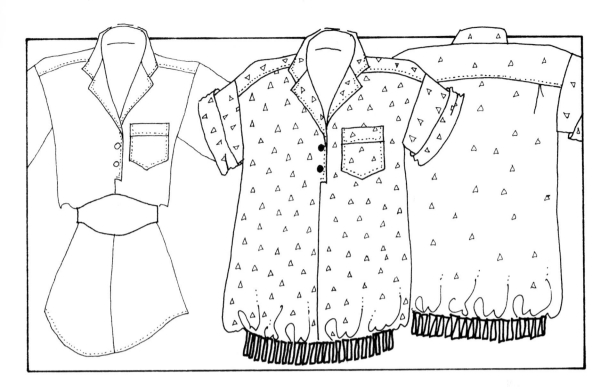

STYLE B ——————————————

This is a very loose-fitting shirt style with a dropped shoulder line and a couple of soft pleats from the back yoke. It has a rever collar, a couple of buttons to fasten the front opening and sleeves which are casually rolled up.

It will be made into a blouson style top with ribbing at the hipline.

1 Trace the yoke, front and back and sleeve patterns and transfer the waist position and all other pattern markings.

2 Add 13mm (½in) parallel to the front and back side seams and to the underarm seams of the sleeve so that it corresponds with the enlarged bodice.

3 On the yoke pattern, draw a line from point A to point B through the shoulder line and cut along this line.

4 Place the yoke sections on a large piece of paper and spread the pattern 2.5cm (1in) apart. Secure pattern to the paper beneath it.

5 Extend the straight line F to B on to point E to give a straight back yoke line.

6 Draw a straight line to connect points C and D to give a straight front yoke line.

Blouson top with hipline ribbing (style B)

13 Style B: original blouse and maternity shape

7 On the front body pattern draw a straight line from mid-yoke seam (point G) to mid-hemline (point H). Cut along this line.

8 Place front pattern sections on a large sheet of paper.

9 Spread the yoke seam 2.5cm (1in) apart at point G and 6.5cm (2½in) apart at the waistline. Secure to the paper beneath.

10 Re-draw the yoke seam from point I to point J with a smooth line.

11 On the back body pattern, mark a point on the centre of the yoke seam (point K) and another on the hemline point mid-way between C.B. and the side (point L). Join point K to point L with a straight line and cut along this line.

12 Lay the back pattern sections on a large sheet of paper and spread point K 2.5cm (1in) apart. Spread the pattern 4cm (1½in) apart at the waistline. Secure to the paper beneath.

13 Re-draw the back yoke seam from point M to point N with a smooth line.

14 Pin the front and back patterns together along the side seams to work on the hemline.

15 Pin the yoke pattern to the back body pattern and measure 66cm (26in) from C.B. neck to the new hemline. This is a good average length for a blouson maternity top.

16 Adjust the front and back hemlines equally.

17 Add 5cm (2in) to the C.F. length to allow for the protrusion of the tummy then join C.F. to C.B. with a smoothly curved line.

18 Add 1.5cm (⅝in) S.A. to the new hemline for attaching the ribbing. Separate the front and back patterns.

19 For a band of ribbing which finishes 6.5cm (2½in) wide, cut a long strip of ribbing 6.5cm (2½in) x 2 = 13cm (5in) + 3cm (1¼in) S.A. – a total width of 16cm (6¼in). Fold the band in half lengthways, and hold it around your low hipline, stretching it slightly to obtain a comfortable fit. Join the ribbing with a seam inside then fold in half lengthways again and attach it to the hem of the blouson with a 1.5cm (⅝in) seam.

20 Use original collar, facing and pocket patterns.

14   Alteration to pattern B

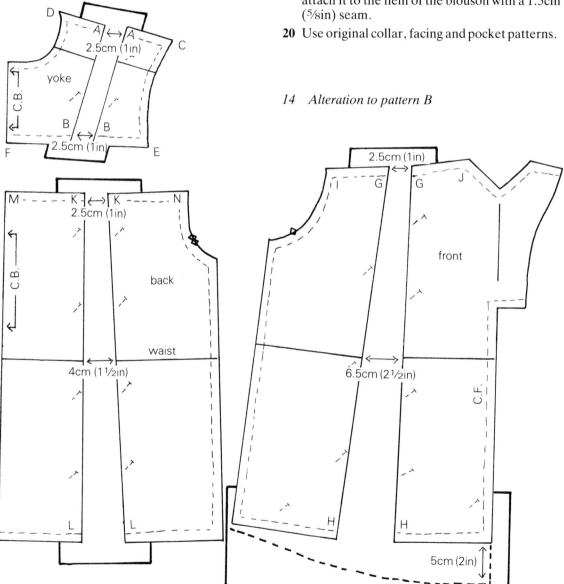

STYLE C _____

A loose-fitting shirt style with soft gathering falling from the front and back yoke. It has long sleeves with gathered sleeve heads, buttons and buttonholes down the front and a pointed shirt collar and collar band. It will be made into a loose shirt-type over-blouse with shirt tails at the hem.

1 Trace around the front, back and sleeve patterns. Transfer the waistline and all pattern markings. The yoke will not be altered as it is a fitted yoke and this original fit must be retained.

2 Add 13mm (½in) parallel to back and front side seams and to the underarm seams of the sleeves. This makes the pattern a size larger.

3 On the front body pattern, mark point A in the centre of the yoke seam. Mark point B on the front hem mid-way between C.F. and the side. Join point A to point B with a straight line and cut along this line.

4 Lay both front sections on a large sheet of paper. Spread the pattern 2.5cm (1in) apart at point A and 7.5cm (3in) apart at the waist. Draw a smooth yoke line from point C to point D.

5 On the back pattern, mark point E mid-way along the yoke seam and point F mid-way along the hem line. Join point E to point F with a straight line and cut along this line.

6 Place both back pattern sections on a large sheet of paper. At point E, spread the pattern 2.5cm (1in) apart and at the waistline 5cm (2in) apart. Draw a smooth back yoke line from point G to point H.

By adding 7.5cm (3in) to the front waist and 5cm (2in) to the back waist, the total waist circumference has been increased by 25cm (10in), which should be sufficient on a loose-fitting shirt. The extra amount added to the yoke seams C-D and G-H will be additional gathering.

15   Style C: the original shirt and the maternity version

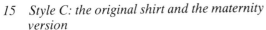

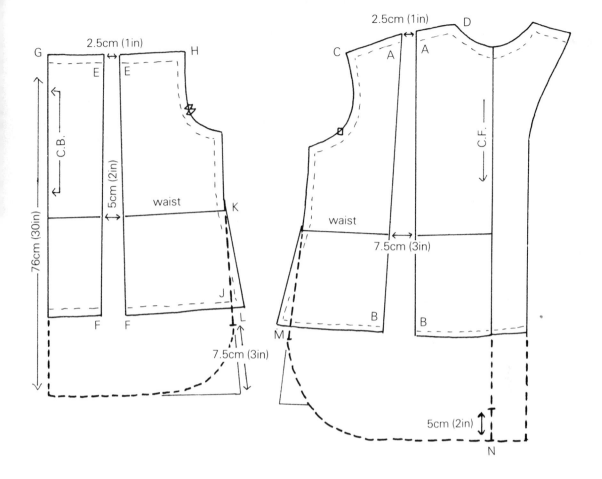

7 As the design of this over-blouse has quite a straight silhouette you will probably want to straighten the side seams by removing some of the flare. Mark point J on the back hemline 13mm (½in) in from the side seam. Join point J to the waistline (point K) with a straight line. Cut along this line from point J to point K and remove this small wedge. Do exactly the same on the front pattern.

8 To determine the new hemline, pin the yoke pattern to the back body pattern. Measure from the back neck 76cm (30in) down the C.B. Add this extra length equally to the back and front hemlines. This is an average length for an over-blouse with shirt tails.

◁ *Loose over-blouse with shirt tails (style C)*

9 On the side seam of the back pattern, mark point L 7.5cm (3in) up from the hem. To form shirt-tails, begin at point L and draw a rounded curve down to the hem.

10 On the front pattern, measure 7.5cm (3in) up the side seam to point M.

11 On the C.F., measure down 5cm (2in) to point N. This is the extra length added to allow for the protrusion of the tummy.

12 Join point M to point N with a smoothly curved line.

13 Add 2cm (¾in) S.A. to both hemlines for a machined hem.

14 Use the original patterns of the yoke, collar, collar band and cuffs.

If you feel adventurous, you could use this same pattern but, instead of gathering, make small tucks and perhaps shorten the sleeve by about 13cm (5in) to give a ¾-length sleeve.

17 Style D: the original blouse and the maternity top

STYLE D _____

This is a basic blouse shape with bust darts. It has no tucks, gathers or yokes. It has been styled on the sailor look with a sailor collar, short sleeves and turned up cuffs with no front or back opening; it will be made into a maternity blouson shape with a drawstring through a channel at the hem.

1 Trace sleeve, front and back patterns, transferring the waistline, darts and other pattern markings.

2 Add 13mm (½in) parallel to front and back side seams and the underarm seams of the sleeves to make the pattern a size larger.

3 On the front pattern, draw a line from the point of the bust dart (point A) down to the hem (point B), keeping it parallel to the C.F.

4 Cut along this line from point B up to point A and place pattern on a large sheet of paper.

5 Fold the underarm bust dart closed, as you would when you sew it, and you will find a huge wedge opens up on the line A-B. Secure the pattern to the paper beneath it.

This will automatically give you the extra fullness you need over the tummy.

6 Extra width must be added to the back pattern so place it on a large sheet of paper and pin the C.B. neck (point C) touching the edge of the paper.

7 Hold point C in place with your finger and swing the back pattern so that point D at the C.B. hem lies 4cm (1½in) away from the straight edge of the paper. Secure in place.

8 Mark point E in the middle of the shoulder seam. Mark point F mid-way along the hem.

9 Join point E to point F with a straight line.

10 Cut from point F up to the stitching line at point E. Do not cut through the shoulder S.A. at point E.

11 Place your finger over point E to hold it in position and open the hem of the pattern 2.5cm (1in) at point F. Secure in place.

12 From point G at the underarm draw a new smooth side seam which extends the waist by 13mm (½in) and point H at the hemline by 2.5cm (1in).

13 The line from point C to point J is now the new C.B. grain and foldline.

26

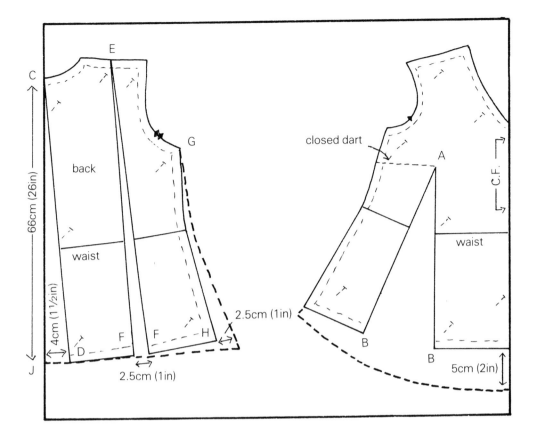

By increasing the front and back with all these wedges, the waist circumference should be sufficiently enlarged. It does not matter that the front pattern is quite a lot wider than the back pattern with this style.

14 Pin the front and back patterns together along the side seams.

15 To obtain the correct length for this blouson shape, measure from C.B. neck 66cm (26in) down the C.B. Add this extra length equally to back and front hems.

16 Extend the C.F. by 5cm (2in) at the hem. This is the allowance added for the protrusion of the tummy. Join the C.B. and the C.F. with a smoothly curved hemline.

17 To form the 2cm (¾in) hem channel through which the drawstring will be threaded add a total of 4.5cm (1¾in) to the hem of the front and back patterns.

When sewing, leave a small opening in the side seam at one side of the channel to allow the drawstring to be threaded through and for the bow to be tied and untied.

18   Alteration to pattern D

STYLE E ————————————————

This is similar to style C as it has a fitted yoke with gathering falling from the yoke at the front and back. It has long full sleeves and a low V-neck with a collar. The yoke, collar, neck facing and cuffs will not be altered.

1 Trace front, back and sleeve patterns marking the waistline and other pattern markings. Add 13mm (½in) parallel to front and back side seams and to the underarm seams of the sleeves to correspond with the enlarged bodice. This makes the pattern a size larger.

2 On the front pattern, mark point E mid-way along the yoke seam A-B.

3 Mark point F on the hemline mid-way between point C and point D.

4 Cut along the line E-F and lay both sections of the front pattern on a large sheet of paper.

5 Spread the yoke 2.5cm (1in) apart at point E and spread the pattern 7.5cm (3in) apart at the waist. Secure to the paper beneath.

6 On the back pattern, mark point K mid-way along the yoke seam G-H.

19 Style E: the original blouse and maternity shape

7 Mark point L on the hemline mid-way between point I and point J.

8 Cut along the line K-L and place the pattern on a large sheet of paper.

9 Spread the pattern 2cm (¾in) apart at point K, and at the waistline spread the pattern 5cm (2in) apart. Secure the pattern to the paper beneath.

In all 25.5cm (10cm) has been added to the waist circumference. This should be adequate for average expansion, but for a looser fit you could spread the pattern further. The increased amounts added to the yoke seams will be used as extra gathers.

10 To determine the new hemline, pin the back yoke pattern to the body section. Measure down the C.B. from the back neck 71cm (28in). This is a good average length for an over-blouse of this type. Add the extra length evenly to front and back hems.

11 Pin front and back patterns together at the side seams. Extend the C.F. downwards by 5cm (2in) to allow for the protrusion of the tummy.

12 Join C.F. to C.B. with a smoothly curved hemline and add an allowance for a hem. Detach front and back patterns.

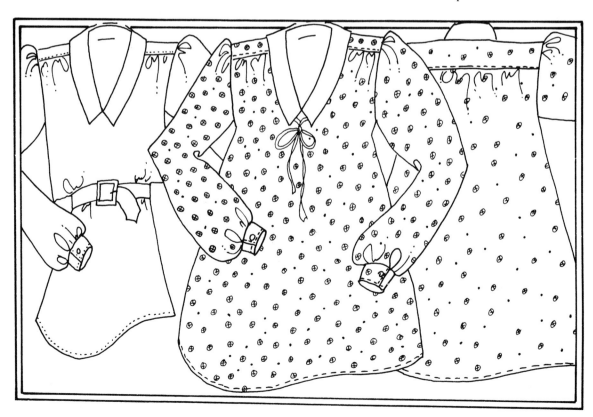

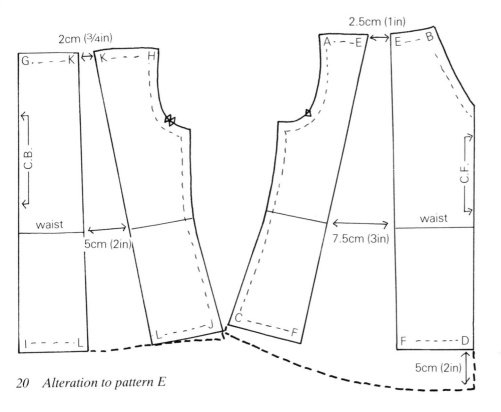

20   *Alteration to pattern E*

STYLE F ─────────────────────────

For the early stages of pregnancy, before your bump appears, but when your everyday clothes are beginning to feel a bit tight around the waist, this skirt would be ideal. It is a very simple, gathered skirt with two large patch pockets and an adjustable elasticated waist.

1 To make the pattern, measure from your waist downwards to find the length you would like your skirt. An average length is 66cm (26in).

2 Measure your waistline and multiply this measurement by 1¾. For example, a 71cm (28in) waist x 1¾ = 124cm (49in). This will be the finished circumference of the new skirt.

3 On a large sheet of paper draw a rectangle 66cm (26in) long and 31cm (12¼in) wide. (This is a quarter of the finished waist circumference as it is only necessary to make a quarter of this skirt pattern.)

4 Mark the corners A, B, C and D as shown.

5 The line A-C will be the C.F. and C.B. grain and foldline.

6 Extend the line C-D by 2.5cm (1in) to point E. Join point E to point B with a straight line. The line B-E is the new side seam and it gives the skirt a bit of necessary flare.

21   *Style F*

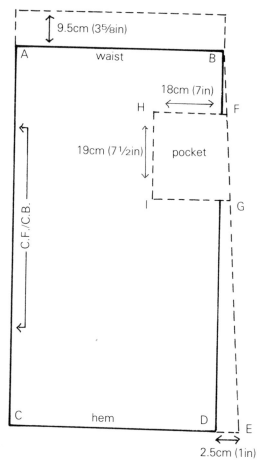

9.5cm (3⅝in)

A   waist   B

18cm (7in)

H   F

19cm (7½in)   pocket

C.F./C.B.

G

C   hem   D   E

2.5cm (1in)

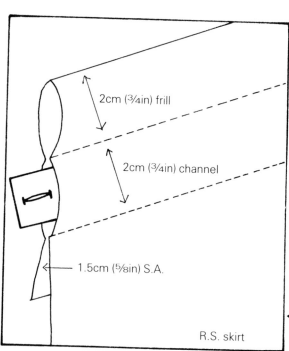

2cm (¾in) frill

2cm (¾in) channel

1.5cm (⅝in) S.A.

R.S. skirt

◁ 22   *Pattern for style F*

7 To position the patch pocket, measure from point B downwards 11.5cm (4½in) to point F.

8 From point F measure downwards 19cm (7½in) to point G.

9 The line F to H is 18cm (7in) long and must run parallel to the waist.

10 At point H, make a 90 degree (right angle) corner and measure 19cm (7½in) down to point I.

11 Connect point I to point G to complete the pocket.

12 Trace the pocket pattern H to F to G to I on another piece of paper and add S.A.s. The pocket will be slightly shaped because of the side seam so do mark your pattern to ensure you attach it to your skirt correctly.

13 At the waist, the pattern must be increased for the waist channel. Add 9.5cm (3⅝in) S.A. to the line A to B.

14 Add S.A. to the hem and 1.5cm (⅝in) S.A. to the side seam.

15 Cut out the finished pattern twice in fabric, both on the fold, once for the front skirt and once for the back.

16 When sewing this skirt, begin by folding the pocket S.A.s back, tracking and pressing them in place then top stitching them to the front skirt.

17 Tack then stitch and neaten both side seams.

18 At the waist, fold to the W.S., measure and tack a hem of 5.5cm (2⅛in).

19 Do a row of top stitching 2cm (¾in) away from the folded edge. This will form a narrow, decorative frill above the channel.

20 Do a second row of top stitching 4cm (1½in) away from the folded edge. This forms a 2cm (¾in) channel. Carefully open the stitching of the side seam at one side of this channel to insert the special buttonhole elastic. Sew a small, flat button to the inside of the channel. (See p. 75).

21 Neaten the 1.5cm (⅝in) S.A. below the channel.

22 Make the hem.

◁ 23   *Waist channel for style F*

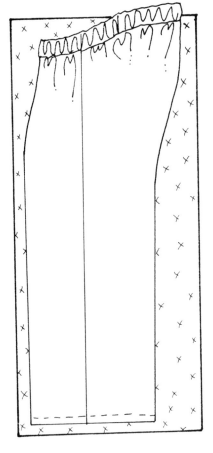

STYLE G _____

Gathered skirts, wrap-around skirts and skirts pleated from the waist may be easy to make, very comfortable and non-restricting to wear, but in the later stages of pregnancy they are not always very flattering from the side view. As the tummy protrudes, the front hem of the skirt is pushed forwards by this protrusion which merely emphasises the tummy, making you appear much larger than you need to.

A skirt which is slim-fitting, but obviously adjusted to cover the tummy and worn with an over-shirt or a blouson top, always gives a much more flattering silhouette.

To make this pattern, you will need to take a few important measurements of your own body.

1 Tie a piece of ribbon or string around your waist to 'fix' your waistline.

2 Measure 20cm (8in) down from the fixed waistline to your hipline. Measure the circumference of your hips at this level and jot the measurement down on a piece of paper. For example, hips for a size 12 measure, on average, 91.5cm (36in).

◁ 24   *Side view of style G*

25   *Pattern for style G*
▽

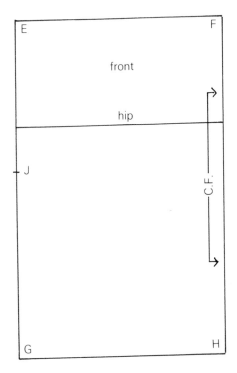

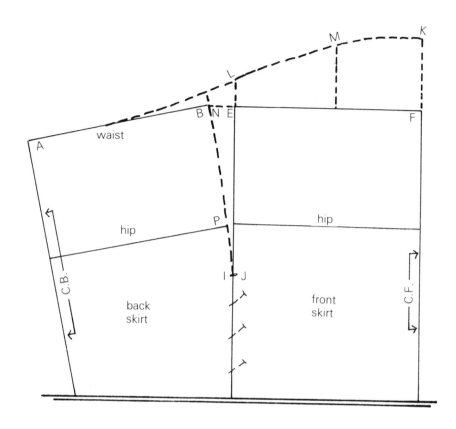

26   Pattern for style G

3 Measure from the fixed waistline downwards to find your finished skirt length. An average length skirt is 66cm (26in) long. Jot this measurement down.

4 To make the pattern, add 18cm (7in) to your hip measurement. For example, size 12 hips of 91.5cm (36in) + 18cm (7in) = 109.5cm (43in).

5 Divide your new total circumference by 4. 109.5cm (43in) ÷ 4 = 27.4cm (10¾in).

6 On large sheets of paper, draw two rectangles exactly the same size and mark them as shown. The rectangles should be 27.4cm (10¾in) wide and 66cm (26in) long.

7 Thigh level is, on average, 32cm (12½in) below the waist and this level must be marked on both rectangles: points I and J.

8 The front rectangle must be extended upwards and outwards to add the necessary fullness.

9 Extend the C.F. line H to F upwards 12cm (4¾in) to point K.

10 Extend the line G to E upwards 4cm (1½in) to point L.

11 Mid-way along the line E to F, extend a line upwards 10cm (4in) to point M.

12 Extend the line F to E sideways by 5cm (2in) to point N.

13 Extend the hip line outwards 1cm (⅜in) to point P.

14 Connect points N, P and J with a smooth curve to form the new front side seam.

15 Pin the back skirt pattern to the front at the side seams so that point N touches point B.

16 Draw a new raised waistline from C.B. curving smoothly up to pass through points L and M to point K.

17 Separate the back and front patterns.

18 Add a hem of 5.5cm (2⅛in) to the waist for an adjustable elasticated channel (see p. 75).

19 Add 1.5cm (⅝in) S.A. to the side seams.

20 Add S.A. to the hems.

This slim-fitting skirt has been made 20cm (8in) larger over the tummy. This would give a good average fit, though if you want a looser fit the width of the original rectangles can be increased.

STYLE H ————————————

The previous pattern is a good slim-fitting skirt but you may decide to be more adventurous and make skirts with more style detail. The pattern of style G is used as the basic pattern from which this skirt is made.

This skirt is pleated from thigh level; when worn with a long overshirt it looks like a fully pleated skirt but will give a more flattering profile. The front tummy area has stretchy fabric over it for extra comfort and extra room for growth.

1 Trace the front and back patterns of style G. Transfer all pattern markings including thigh level.

2 On the C.F. line A-B measure downwards 24cm (9½in) to point E.

3 On the side seam of the front pattern C-D measure downwards 7.5cm (3in) to point F.

4 Connect point F to point E with a smoothly curved line then cut along this line.

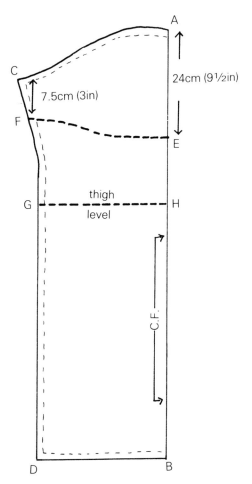

28   Pattern for style H

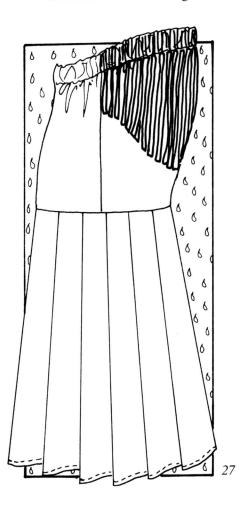

27   Style H

5 The pattern section C to A to E to F will be cut out in stretchy fabric for extra comfort. Add 1.5cm (⅝in) S.A. to the lower edge F-E so that you can attach it to the body of the skirt. Remember that the waist and side seam already have S.A.s and the C.F. will be placed on the fold of your stretchy fabric.

6 Cut off the front pattern at thigh level, along the line G-H. Add 1.5cm (⅝in) S.A. to this seam and also to the seam F to E, which will be attached to the stretchy panel.

7 Cut off the back pattern at thigh level like the front and add 1.5cm (⅝in) S.A.

8 To find out how much fabric you will need for the pleating measure the circumference of your pattern at thigh level. For example, on an average size 12 this will be 109.5cm (43in). Multiply this length by 3. 109.5cm (43in) x 3 = 328.5cm (149in). You will need to join widths of fabric to obtain this width.

9 The length of these pleats will be the measurement from thigh level to your original hem. For example, for a 66cm (26in) long skirt the length of the pleating will be 34cm (13½in). Add 1.5cm (⅝in) S.A. to the top of the pleated section and a hem allowance to the lower edge.

10 When sewing this skirt, begin on the front by joining the stretchy section to the body section.

11 Join the front and back skirts at the side seams and neaten them.

12 Make the waist channel and insert adjustable buttonhole elastic.

13 Measure and pin the pleating evenly and attach it to the skirt. Sew the hem.

This method will give the fullest pleating and the pleats can be left to hang softly or be pressed in place. If you want to use less fabric you could make less full pleats.

STYLE I

The basic slim-fitting skirt on p. 31 can be used again in a slightly different way. This skirt has an area completely cut away over the tummy; the adjustable buttonhole elastic sits above the tummy to support the skirt. This style has a decorative back opening with large buttons.

1 Trace the front and back patterns of style G.

2 On the C.F. line A-B measure downwards 24cm (9½in) to point D.

3 On the front waist measure from point A towards point C 9cm (3½in) to point E.

4 Join point E to point D with a smooth curve. Cut along this line. This is the U-shaped area cut out over the tummy and, when sewing the skirt, its edges will be neatened with a binding, a pin hem or a narrow facing. Add appropriate S.A.s.

29 *Side and back views of style I*

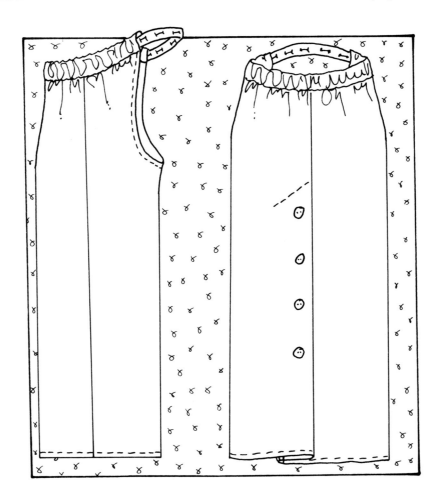

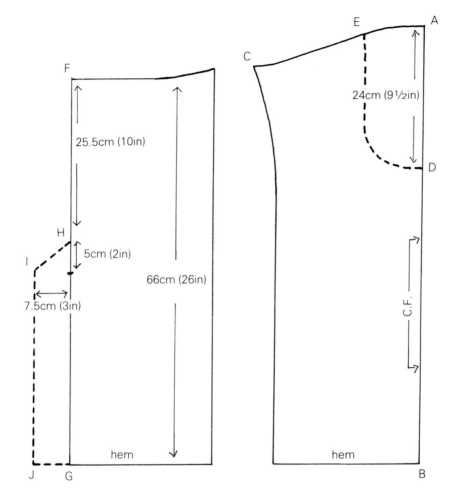

5 On the back pattern, measure downwards from point F 25.5cm (10in) to point H.

6 Measure 5cm (2in) down from point H and outwards 7.5cm (3in) to find point I.

7 Draw a line from point I down to hem level (point J) keeping it parallel to the C.B.

8 Add 1.5cm (⅝in) S.A. to the back seam and decorative pleat from point F to H to I to J, then complete the hem to point G.

9 Large buttons can be stitched on this back pleat for decoration.

30 Pattern for style I

STYLE J _____

This is a very simple dress made from the T-shirt pattern used for style A. This high 'waistline' gives a smooth and flattering fit to the bodice and the soft pleats are placed exactly where they are needed – over the bump!

It could be made in a plain or printed cotton fabric for summer wear or in a fine wool or needlecord and worn over a jersey for winter.

31   Style J

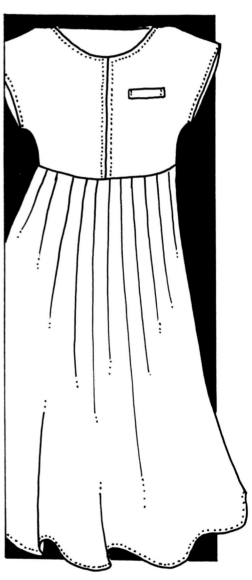

◁ *Simple, yet flattering, dress adapted from a T-shirt pattern (style J)*

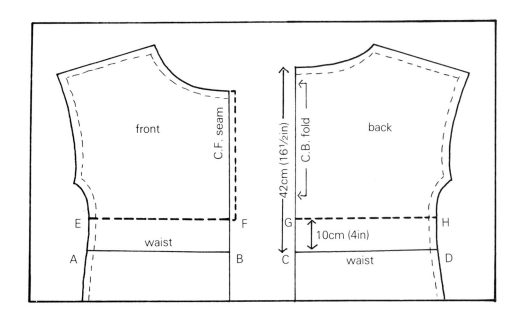

1 Trace the front and back patterns, transferring the waist position and other pattern markings.

2 Add 13mm (½in) parallel to front and back side seams to make it a size larger.

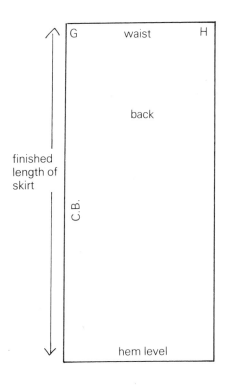

3 To find the new high 'waistline', measure upwards 10cm (4in) from the waist of the pattern and draw lines E-F and G-H. This is the new high 'waistline'.

4 Add 1.5cm (⅝in) S.A. to the new high waistline then cut off and discard the lower section of the pattern.

5 Add 1.5cm (⅝in) S.A. to the C.F. to make a seam for decorative purposes.

6 To make the skirt patterns you must decide on the finished length you want your dress to be from point G to the hem.

7 On large sheets of paper, draw two rectangles. The rectangle for the front pattern will be the width of E-F and the length of the finished skirt. The back rectangle will be the width of G-H and the length of the finished skirt. Mark the C.F. and the C.B.

8 On the front pattern, extend the line K-J by 2.5cm (1in) to point L. Join point L to point E to give slight flare to the side seam.

9 Extend the line E-F by 20cm (8in) to point M. Draw the line M-N parallel to the line F-K. This adds fullness to your skirt pattern for the pleating. The line M-N is your new C.F. grain and foldline.

10 Repeat steps 7, 8 and 9 with the back skirt rectangle.

11 Add 1.5cm (⅝in) S.A. to the waist and side seams of front and back skirts.

12 Lengthen the C.F. line M-N by 5cm (2in) and from this point draw a smoothly curved hemline up to point L to allow for the protrusion of the tummy.

13 Add an allowance for a hem to front and back hemlines.

When sewing this dress, make the bodice and topstitch the neck and C.F. seam, then join the side seams of the front and back skirts. Measure and pin soft pleats all around the top of the skirt then attach the skirt to the bodice. Neaten the hem. Add a small decorative pocket if you want to.

Several blouse shapes can be equally successfully used to make maternity dresses by this method and the skirt could be gathered onto the bodices instead of being pleated.

_____

STYLE K _____

The style of this dress is based on blouse style B – a very casual blouson top with a band of stretchy ribbing on the hips. To make the dress, a softly gathered skirt is attached to the lower edge of the ribbing.

1 Follow steps 1 to 18 of style B.

2 Cut a long strip of stretchy ribbing 8cm (3¼in) wide and place it around your body at hip level, stretching it slightly to obtain a comfortable fit. Mark this length carefully with pins.

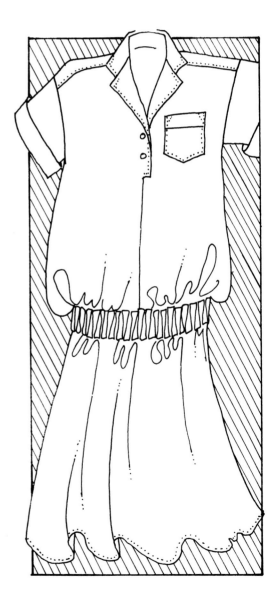

34   Style K

3 To make the skirt pattern, measure your hips 20cm (8in) below your waist and jot this measurement down on paper. Measure the finished length you would like your dress to be from hip level to hem and write this down also.

4 Multiply your hip measurement by 1½ to obtain the circumference of your skirt. For example, a hip measurement of 96.5cm (38in) x 1½ = 144.8cm (47in).

5 The skirt pattern will be a rectangle. Its depth will be the finished length of your skirt and its width will be 1½ x your hip measurement. You may need to join two widths of fabric when cutting it out in fabric as it is a very wide pattern.

6 Add 1.5cm (⅝in) S.A. to all skirt edges and add an allowance for a hem. (The hem of this skirt is straight as extra length to allow for the protrusion of the tummy has been added to the bodice.)

When sewing this dress, make the bodice completely. Stretch and attach the ribbing with a 1.5cm (⅝in) S.A. to the bodice. Make the skirt, gather its top edge and attach it to the lower edge of the ribbing, stretching the ribbing as you sew.

— — — — — — — — — — — — — — —

STYLE L — — — — — — — — — — — —

This shirt dress is based on blouse style C. Once the hard work has been done altering your everyday shirt pattern into a maternity top, it is extremely easy to lengthen this into a smart dress.

1 Follow steps 1 to 14 of style C.

2 Decide on a finished length for your dress and measure from your waistline to your hem. For example, an average size 12 waist to hem would be 61cm (24in).

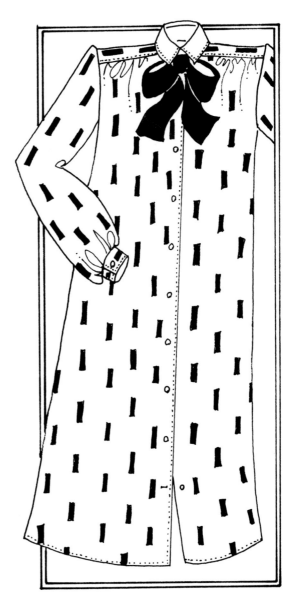

35 Style L

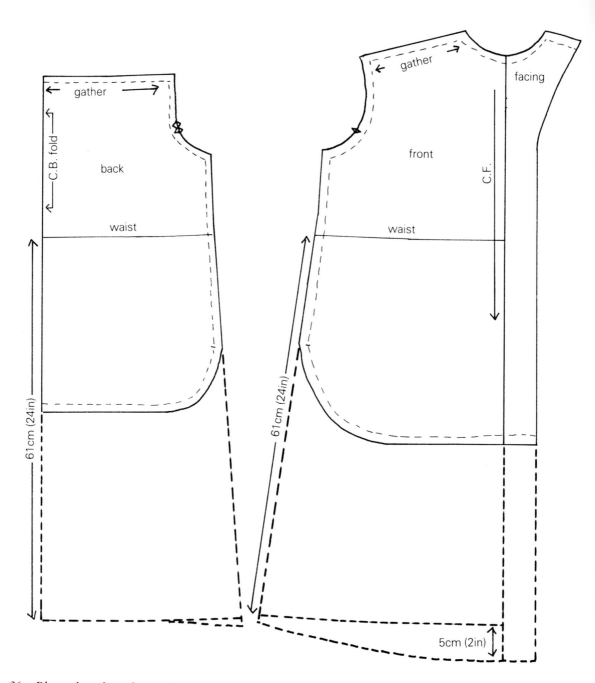

36 *Blouse lengthened to make style L*

3 On the back pattern, extend the C.B. foldline 61cm (24in). Extend the side seam by the same length. Draw the new hemline.

4 On the front pattern extend the C.F. by 61cm (24in) + 5cm (2in) for the tummy protrusion. Extend the side seam by 61cm (24in). Draw the front hem with a smooth curve.

5 Add a hem allowance to front and back hems.

STYLE M

This is a pretty dress with a very deep hem frill. It is based on blouse style E.

1 Follow steps 1 to 12 of style E.

2 Decide on the finished length you want your dress to be and how deep you want the hem frill. For example, for an average size 12 dress with a C.B. length of 104cm (41in), the frill should be 35cm (14in) deep.

3 On a scrap of paper, write down the finished length of your dress. Subtract the depth of your frill and you will get the length of the body of your dress.

| If dress length is | 104cm (41in) |
| and frill depth is | 35cm (14in) |

| then the body of the dress will be | 69cm (27in) long |

4 Adjust the length of front and back patterns equally and add 1.5cm (⅝in) S.A. for attaching the frill.

5 To make the frill pattern, measure the lower edges of the front and back patterns A-B and C-D. As this is only half a pattern, multiply by two to get the full hem circumference. For example, on a size 12 pattern the hem circumference is about 137cm (54in).

6 The frill pattern will be a rectangle. Its depth will be 35cm (14in) and its width, to allow for the gathers, will be 1¾ x 137cm (54in) = 240cm (95in). You may need to join two or three widths of fabric when cutting it out as it is a very wide pattern.

37 Style M

41

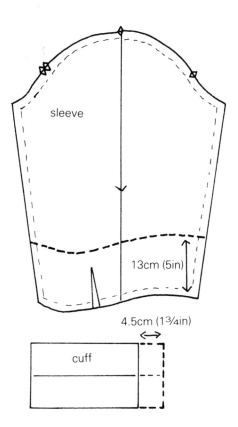

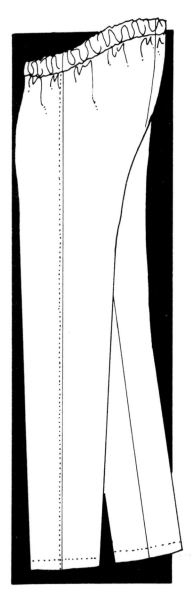

STYLE N ⎯⎯⎯⎯⎯⎯⎯⎯⎯⎯⎯⎯

The everyday trouser pattern used for this style has two pleats on either side of the C.F. zip opening, side pockets and two darts on either side of the C.B.

1 On large sheets of paper, trace around the back and front patterns ignoring all waist darts and pleats. Transfer the grain lines and hip level 20cm (8in) below the waist.

2 To make the pattern a size larger, 13mm (½in) is added parallel to front and back side seams from the waist to thigh level – 32cm (12½in) down and then gradually tapered in to the original hemline to give a smooth side seam.

38   Shorten sleeve and lengthen cuff for ¾-length sleeve

7 Add 1.5cm (⅝in) S.A. to the top and sides of the frill pattern and also an allowance for the hem. This hemline is straight as the extra length necessary for the protrusion of the tummy has been added to the body section of the dress.

8 To make the sleeves ¾-length, shorten the sleeve length by 13cm (5in) and lengthen the cuff by 4.5cm (1¾in).

◁ *Pretty dress with a very deep hem frill (style M)*

⎯ ⎯ ⎯ ⎯ ⎯ ⎯ ⎯ ⎯ ⎯ ⎯ ⎯ ⎯ ⎯

39   Style N

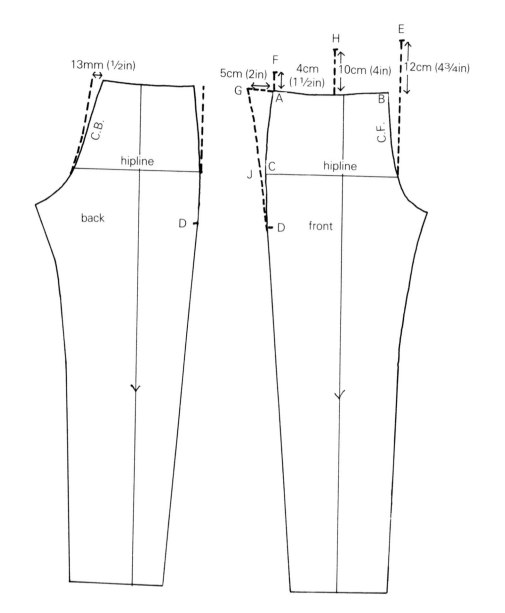

3 On the back pattern, increase the C.B. waist by 13mm (½in) and draw a new C.B. seamline. Straighten the side seam above hip level so that it lies parallel to the grain line.

4 On the front pattern, straighten the C.F. seam above hip level, so that it lies parallel to the grain line, and extend the C.F. upwards 12cm (4¾in) to point E.

5 Extend point A upwards 4cm (1½in) to point F.

6 Extend point A sideways 5cm (2in) to point G.

7 Midway along the line A-B, extend upwards 10cm (4in) to point H.

8 At point C extend the hipline outwards 1cm (⅜in) to point J.

9 Draw a new smoothly curved side seam from point D at thigh level through point J to point G.

10 Pin back and front patterns together along the side seams. From the C.B., draw a new waistline passing through point F and H to point E at the C.F.

11 Separate front and back patterns adding 1.5cm (⅝in) S.A. where necessary and also adding an allowance for the waist channel through which to thread the adjustable buttonhole elastic.

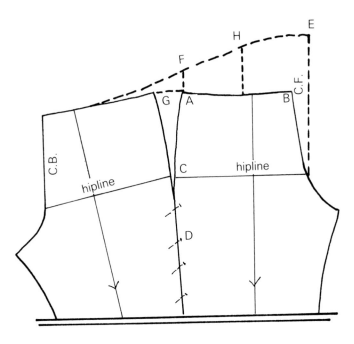

STYLE O —

These knickerbockers are based on style N. They could be made in rich velvet or crêpe-de-chine for party wear or in needlecord or cotton drill for daywear. They would be a fun addition to your wardrobe.

1 Follow steps 1 to 11 of style N.

2 Decide on the length of your knickerbockers – they should end just below the knee. For example, an average size 12 pair of knickerbockers would have an inside leg measurement of about 46cm (18in).

3 On the front pattern, measure 46cm (18in) down the inside leg seam and draw the new hem. Add a hem allowance of 5cm (2in).

4 Repeat step 3 on the back pattern.

When sewing these knickerbockers, sew and neaten the inside leg seams and the side seams. Join the left and right legs by sewing then neatening the crotch seam from C.B. around to C.F. Turn over and sew the waist channel and insert adjustable buttonhole elastic (see p. 75). At the hems turn up 5cm (2in), neaten the raw edge then do several rows of shirring 1cm (⅜in) apart to elasticate or sew a channel and insert elastic.

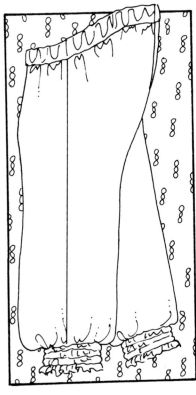

42 *Style O*

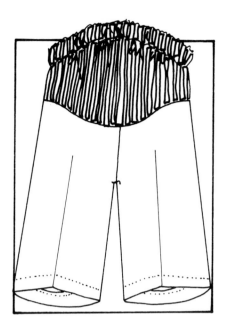

43 Style P

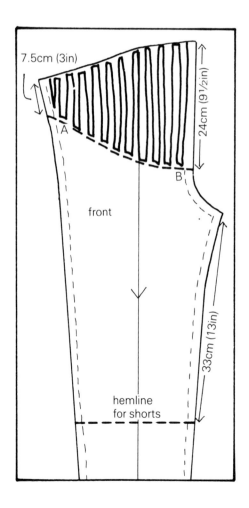

7.5cm (3in)

A

front

24cm (9½in)

B

33cm (13in)

hemline
for shorts

STYLE P ————————————————

These Bermuda shorts are a wonderful asset to a summer maternity wardrobe. They could be made in cotton drill or poplin and worn with a huge T-shirt or brightly printed overshirt. The pattern is based on Style N.

1 Follow steps 1 to 11 of Style N.

2 Measure your inside leg and decide how long you want your shorts to be. For example, an average size 12 pair of Bermuda shorts would have an inside leg measurement of 33cm (13in).

3 On the front pattern measure 33cm (13in) down the inside leg seam and draw the new hemline. Add a hem allowance.

4 Repeat step 3 on the back pattern.

For extra comfort and room for growth you might like to insert a section of stretchy ribbing over the tummy. To do this measure 7.5cm (3in) down the side seam to point A and measure 24cm (9½in) down the C.F. to point B.

Join point A to point B with a smoothly curved line. Cut along this line A-B and add 1.5cm (⅝in) S.A. to both edges.

Remember to place the ribbed section on the fold at C.F. when cutting it out in fabric.

◁ 44 Pattern for Bermuda shorts with ribbed front panel

STYLE Q ————————————————

During pregnancy, jogging pants are very comfortable to wear as they are soft and stretchy. The only problem is that the elasticated waist becomes increasingly uncomfortable around your tummy as you grow, so the best solution is to make yourself a pair with a raised waistline. 'Jogging suit' material and ribbing are easily obtainable in good fabric shops. The pattern is based on trouser style N.

1 Follow steps 1 to 11 of style N.

2 Reduce the width of the leg from thigh level down to the hem on both the side seams and the inside leg seam.

3 Shorten the front and back patterns at the hem remembering that you are going to attach a 5cm (2in) wide band of ribbing around the ankles.

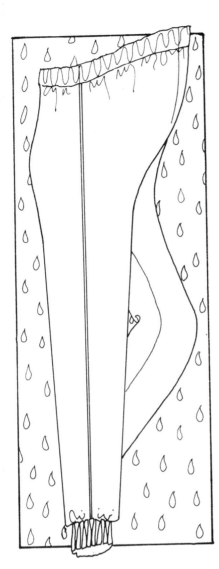

45   *Style Q*

STYLE R ━ ━ ━ ━ ━ ━ ━ ━ ━ ━

This jumpsuit pattern has a plain body with no yokes or tucks or gathers, but with a dropped shoulder line and long sleeves.

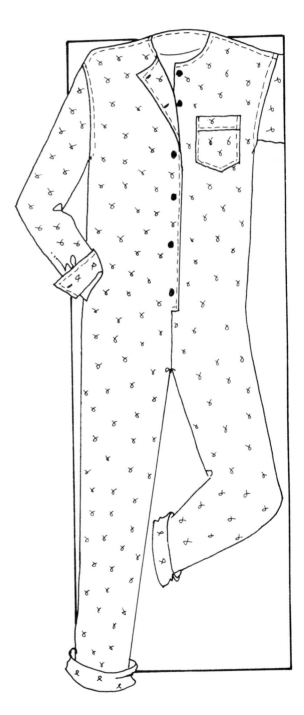

46   *Style R*

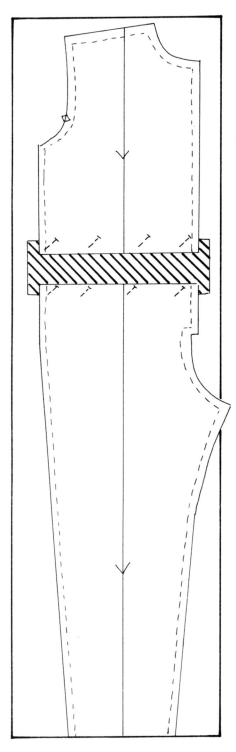

1 Trace the front, back and sleeve patterns onto sheets of paper. Add 13mm (½in) to the side seams of the front and back from underarm to thigh level (approximately 32cm [12½in] below the waist) then taper this line smoothly in to the hemline. Add 13mm (½in) to the underarm seams of the sleeves to make them correspond to the body of the pattern. This makes the pattern a size larger.

2 When worn unbelted the waist of this everyday size 12 commercial pattern was measured and it was 66cm (26in) larger than a size 12 waistline. This should be wide enough for an average pregnancy. If a looser fit is required just add more to the side seams tapering down to the original hem.

3 To allow for the protrusion of the tummy, extra length needs to be added to the body length.

4 Cut front and back patterns through their waistlines and add 5cm (2in) length.

For the first few months of pregnancy you may feel more comfortable wearing this jumpsuit with a loose belt, so remember to make one.

_____

47   *Style R – lengthen jumpsuit pattern by 5cm (2in)*

◁ *Simple jumpsuit with dropped shoulder line and long sleeves (style R)*

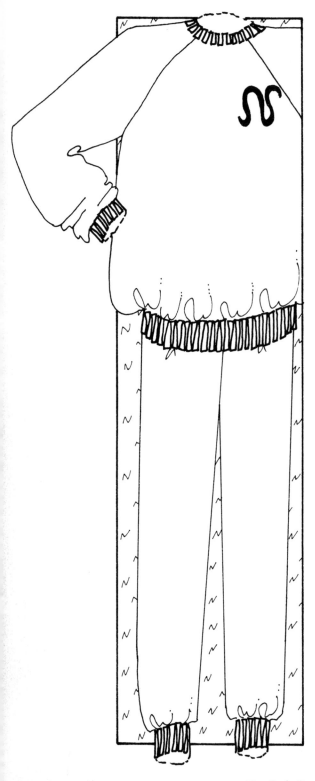

STYLE S _ _ _ _ _ _ _ _ _ _ _ _ _ _ _

A jogging suit is a very comfortable outfit during pregnancy for casual wear or for just lounging about in. The tops of ready-made jogging suits are often not long enough to cover your tummy, and the trousers are uncomfortable as, even though they are wide enough, the elasticated waist sits around the centre of your tummy – just where you don't want it! Now that all the proper fabrics and ribbing are available, why not make your own and be comfortable?

1 Trace the sleeve, front and back patterns and transfer the waistline position and other pattern markings.

2 Add 13mm (½in) parallel to back and front side seams and also to the underarm seams of the sleeve. This makes the pattern a size larger.

3 Place the front pattern on a large sheet of paper.

4 Draw a straight line from point A to point B which extends 2cm (¾in) beyond the C.F. at the waistline. This line forms the new C.F. grain and foldline.

5 Draw a line C to D through the centre of the pattern. Cut from point D up to point C but do not cut through the S.A. at point C.

6 Spread the pattern at point D until the waistline is 2.5cm (1in) apart. Secure the pattern to the sheet of paper beneath.

7 Draw a new smooth side seam from point E to point F extending the waistline by 2cm (¾in).

8 Place the back pattern on a large sheet of paper.

9 Draw a straight line from point G to point H which extends 13mm (½in) beyond the C.B. at the waistline. This line forms the new C.B. grain and foldline.

10 Draw a line I to J through the centre of the pattern. Cut from point J up to point I but do not cut through the S.A. at point I.

11 Spread the pattern at point J until the waistline is 13mm (½in) apart. Secure pattern to the paper beneath.

12 Draw a new smooth side seam from point K to point L extending the waistline by 13mm (½in).

48   Style S

Comfortable jogging suit (style S) ▷

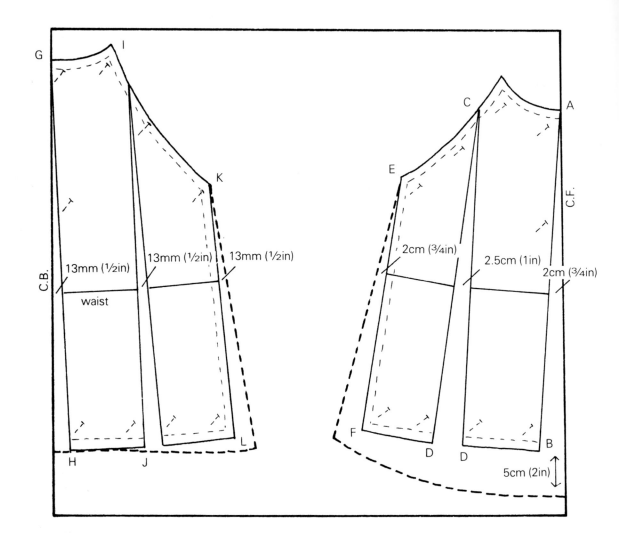

49　Pattern for style S

The circumference of the waist has been increased by a total of 20cm (8in), which should be sufficient on an already baggy jogging top.

13 To find the hem level, measure 68.5cm (27in) down the C.B. from the neck. Increase the back and front hems equally to this length.

14 Extend the C.F. by 5cm (2in). This is the allowance added for the protrusion of the tummy.

15 Pin the front and back together at the side seams and join the C.F. and the C.B. with a smoothly curved hemline.

16 Add 1.5cm (⅝in) S.A. to front and back hems to enable the ribbing to be attached. Separate front and back patterns.

The neckline does not need to be altered from its original size.

To adjust the jogging pants follow the instructions on p. 46.

___

STYLE T _ _ _ _ _ _ _ _ _ _ _ _ _

This is an extremely simple nightie – one size fits everyone. It would be comfortable to wear before the baby is born, and has a slit front opening which would be ideal for breast-feeding the baby in hospital and at home afterwards.

Because so many cotton printed fabrics, which would be ideal for this nightie, are made 90cm (36in) wide the pattern is worked out on this width. You will need 2m (2¼ yd) of 90cm (36in) wide fabric and 2m (2¼ yd) of cord for the drawstring.

50   Style T

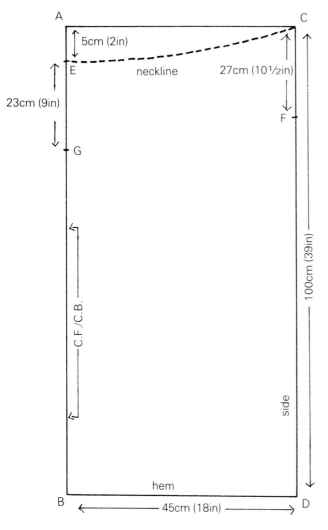

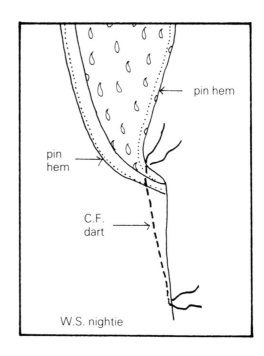

52 To neaten C.F. slit of style T

To cut out this nightie, fold the fabric in half along its length with selvages together.

Place the line E to B along the folded edge and the line C to D along the selvages. Cut out this pattern twice, once for the back and again for the front. On the C.F. fold cut the slit from the neckline at point E down to point G. This forms the C.F. slit opening.

To sew this nightie, make a pin hem around the C.F. slit and stitch a tiny dart at the base of the slit to strengthen it (see diagram 52).

Stitch both side seams 1.5cm (⅝in) wide from point D at the hem up to point F and fasten off securely. Turn back and press 1.5cm (⅝in) S.A. at the armholes and top stitch in place.

At the neckline fold over a 6mm (¼in) hem, then another 2cm (¾in) and top stitch in place to form the neck channel. Thread the cord through the back channel and through both front channels with the ends coming out at the C.F. slit for tying into a bow.

Make a narrow machined hem.

_____

*(left) Simple nightie wtih slit front opening for ▷
breast feeding (style T) and (right) adaptable
nightie/sundress with bustline shirring (style U)*

51 Pattern for style T

1 On a large sheet of paper, draw a rectangle 100cm (39in) long by 45cm (18in) wide and mark the corners A, B, C and D as shown.

2 Measure 5cm (2in) down from point A to point E. Connect point E to point C with a smoothly curved line. This is the neckline, so cut along this line and discard the upper section.

3 Measure down from point C 27cm (10½in) to point F for the armhole slit.

4 Measure 23cm (9in) down from point E to point G for the C.F. slit opening.

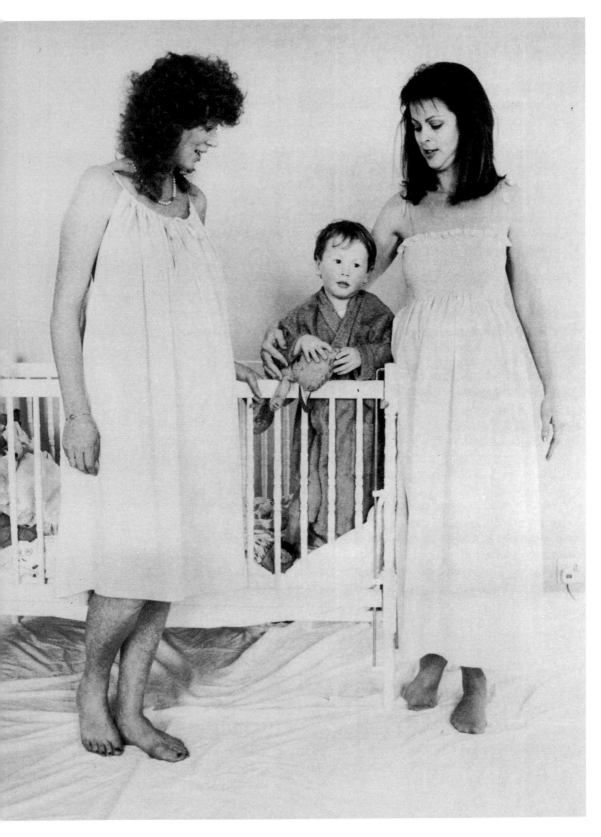

STYLE U _____

This is a simple style which makes an extremely comfortable nightie, and because of all the rows of elasticated shirring it gives a bit of support to the bustline. It can be made long or short, in warm Viyella or in cool cotton lawn. It could also be made as a summer sundress. One size fits everyone.

1 Using 90cm (36in) wide fabric cut out the two lengths necessary for the nightie. For a short nightie, cut each length 75cm (29½in). For a long nightie cut each length 114cm (45in).

2 Join two of the selvages with a 1.5cm (⅝in) seam. Press this new side seam open.

3 Make a small pin hem to neaten the top edge.

4 Begin the rows of elasticated shirring 2cm (¾in) below the pin hem; this gives a tiny frill above the shirring.

5 Using shirring elastic do several rows of shirring 1cm (⅜in) apart to a depth of about 15cm (6in) from one selvage, across the side seam to the other selvage and fasten off securely. If it is not really securely fastened off the shirring will all come apart when you wear the nightie.

Do experiment with the tension of the shirring to make sure that you have got it tight enough or loose enough and just as you want it.

6 Sew the second side seam 1.5cm (⅝in) from the selvage.

7 Make a narrow machined hem.

8 Attach narrow straps of ribbon or cord.

_____

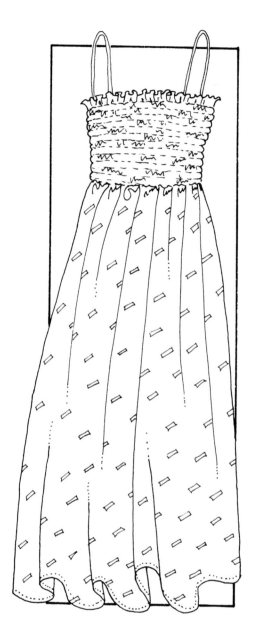

53   Style U

The author wishes to thank Helen Stanley for her valuable help and advice.

56

3. Cutting Out

Once the pattern is complete, the next step is cutting out the fabric. Unless you already happen to have a suitable length of material, you will need to buy some; since fabrics are so expensive these days it is worthwhile working out a rough estimate of the amount needed before going shopping.

54   Cutting-out equipment

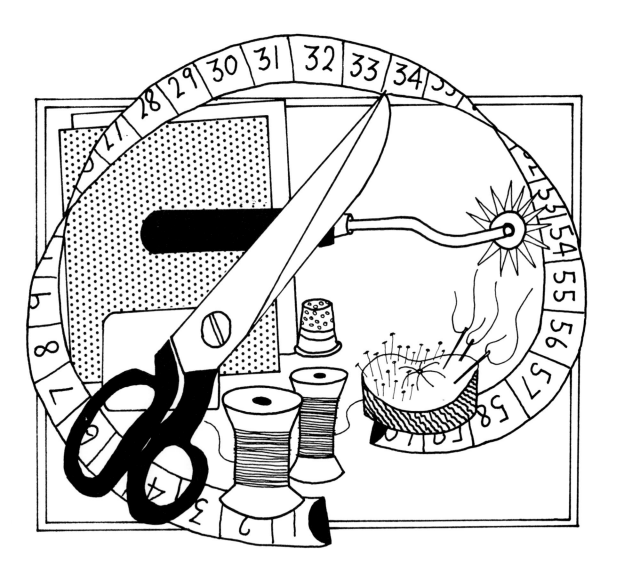

The three most usual widths of fabrics are 90cm (36in), 114cm (45in) and 152cm (60in). If you have a certain fabric in mind and therefore know its

55   Layout with fabric folded on lengthwise grain
▽

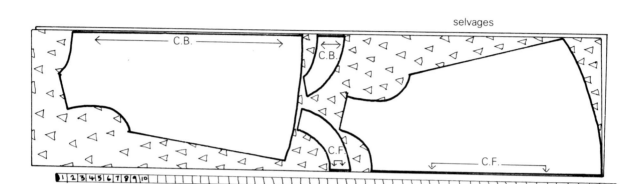

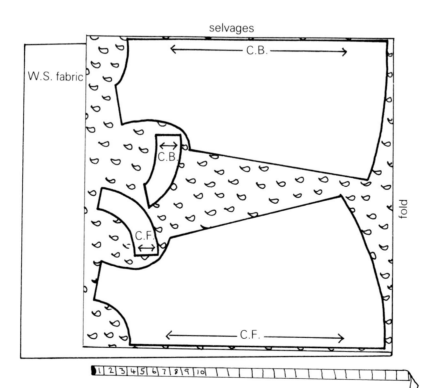

△

56   Layout with fabric folded on crosswise grain

width, then you need only do one quick estimate; otherwise, it is advisable to do a rough estimate on all three widths.

Doing an estimate is a bit like a jigsaw puzzle: all the pieces are carefully slotted in together within the fabric width, and the more carefully it is done, the less fabric is wasted. You may find that, as you are using quite large pattern pieces with maternity clothes, it is more economical to use wider fabrics, as this allows a greater area for slotting in larger pattern pieces. Because only the right half of a pattern is made, you must remember that each pattern piece will be cut out through two layers of fabric to give a full garment, and therefore estimates are made on folded fabric. The way in which the fabric is folded depends on its width and the size and shape of the pattern pieces. The usual method is to fold the fabric in half along its lengthwise grain so the selvages lie on top of each other. This is an especially good method for garments with a C.F. or C.B. fold as the pattern pieces can be laid directly on the fold of the fabric. With larger pattern pieces it may be more economical to fold the fabric along its crosswise grain with selvages on both sides.

On a large, clear surface, such as a big table or the floor, mark out the fabric width using two parallel lengths of string. Lay on all the pattern pieces, positioning them as economically as possible within the measured width and keeping all grain lines parallel to the lengthwise edge. Do not be tempted to turn some pattern pieces around onto the crosswise grain; this would be false economy as these sections would not hang properly on the finished garment. Measure the length of fabric needed when you are satisfied with the positioning of your pieces, and make a rough sketch so that you remember the layout.

EQUIPMENT

To ensure trouble-free cutting out, it is a good idea to collect all the necessary equipment together before beginning. The tools you will need are as follows.

Dressmakers' shears. These should be about 20cm (8in) long with bent handles so that the blades lie flat on the cutting table. They must be kept exclusively for cutting fabric, as cutting paper will dull the blades.

Dressmakers' steel pins and pincushion.

Tape measure.

Iron, ironing board and press cloth.

Tracing wheel and selection of coloured dressmakers' carbon paper.

Tailors' chalk or chalk pencil.

Needle and tacking cotton.

Thimble. This should fit snugly on the middle finger of your sewing hand.

FABRIC PREPARATION

It is important to prepare fabric carefully prior to cutting out as it would be a shame, after all your hard work, to end up with a distorted garment or one which shrank with the first wash. Begin by checking whether or not the length of material is lying exactly on grain, as no finished garment will hang correctly if it is not.

Woven fabric is made by weaving softer threads, called crosswise or weft threads, back and forth between the strong, lengthwise, warp or selvage threads. These should be interwoven at an angle of 90 degrees to each other to be perfectly 'on grain'. Often, due to a weaving fault or, more often, during one of the finishing processes, this angle becomes distorted and the fabric becomes 'off grain'. This is easily noticed on large, woven check fabrics where the checks look more diamond shaped than square.

To find out if fabric is on grain, make a short cut with the points of your scissors through the selvage near the cut end of the length of fabric. Carefully pull out a crosswise thread then cut along this line. Fold the fabric sideways in half with both selvages lying exactly on top of each other. If the cut edge matches evenly when folded then the fabric is perfectly on grain. If it does not then it must be rectified by opening the folded fabric and pulling it firmly on the bias grain until the distorted threads are lying back in position.

Some fabrics do, unfortunately, shrink during their first wash so it is a good idea to test for shrinkage prior to cutting out. Using a needle and tacking thread, tack the outline of a 20cm (8in) square at one end of the fabric then iron this area through a damp press cloth. Re-measure the tacked square. If it has obviously shrunk then you must press the entire length of fabric with a damp press cloth or, if the fabric is washable, dip the length in a basin of warm water then hang it out to dry. Whichever method is used, do ensure that the fabric is perfectly dry before cutting out and give it a good iron on the W.S. to remove all creases. Finally, smooth out any creases on the paper pattern with a cool iron.

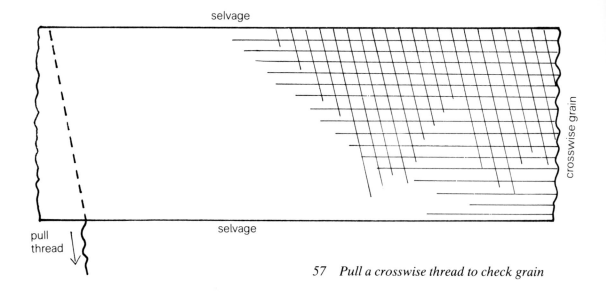

57 Pull a crosswise thread to check grain

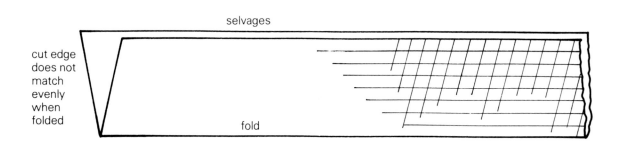

58 Folded fabric is off grain

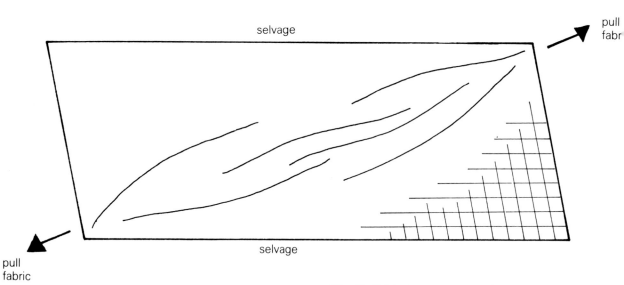

59 Pull fabric to correct grain

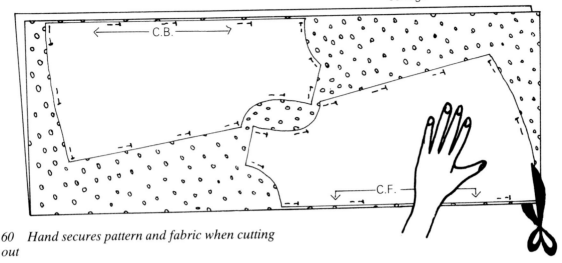

60 *Hand secures pattern and fabric when cutting out*

CUTTING OUT

Lay the prepared fabric on your cutting surface and refer to your layout sketch to remind yourself how to fold the fabric and how to position the pattern pieces. Begin attaching the pattern pieces by the fold of the fabric, if there are to be pieces on the fold. Smooth the pattern and material outwards from the fold with your hand as you go to ensure all the layers are kept flat. Insert pins parallel to the cutting edge within the S.A.s and about 12cm (5in) apart. By pinning within the S.A. there is no risk of pinholes marking the finished garment. Use long, continuous strokes of the shears when cutting around the pieces, as short, snipped cutting leaves ragged edges, and do use your free hand to hold the section you are cutting flat on the table. Cut all notches outwards from the seams so they do not weaken the seam allowances; they can easily be trimmed away later when the seams are neatened.

TRANSFERRING PATTERN MARKINGS

There are several pattern markings that must be carefully transferred to the cut fabric before the paper pattern is unpinned and removed. These include vital markings such as bust darts, pocket positions, tucks, buttons and buttonhole positions, and stitching lines. Depending on the type of fabric being used and the amount of marking needed, you can decide which marking method is most suitable.

The speediest method is to use a tracing wheel and dressmakers' carbon paper of a similar colour to the fabric. This is always done on the W.S. of the fabric, but, even so, must be tested on a scrap beforehand to ensure the carbon does not show through on the R.S. nor do the spikes damage the fabric. When tracing long, straight lengths, it is helpful to run the tracing wheel down the edge of a ruler as you go to ensure a straight line. If you have cut the pieces in pairs do remember to place carbon on both wrong sides and mark them together.

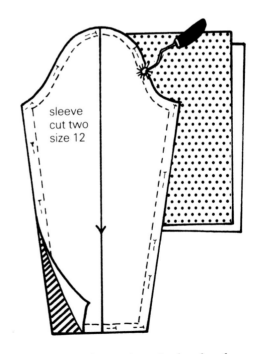

sleeve
cut two
size 12

61 *Marking with a tracing wheel and carbon paper*

Tracing would not be a suitable marking method for very sheer materials, exotic evening fabrics or loosely woven ones, but tailors' tacking would be a good alternative. Using a needle and double, contrasting cotton thread, make a row of tacking stitches along the line which needs to be marked. Instead of pulling the tacking cotton taut between each stitch, leave a loop. When all this tacking is complete, gently remove the pattern then slowly separate the two layers of fabric, snipping the threads between them as you go. As non-slippery, tacking cotton has been used, this marking should remain in place until the garment has been machined; it can then be easily removed with a clothes brush or pair of tweezers.

To mark a single point, such as the point of a dart or the corner of a pocket, a single tailors' tack is needed. Using double tacking cotton in the needle, make a tiny stitch through all layers over the point, followed by a couple more stitches directly on top. Leave a loop between each stitch; this is snipped open when the fabric layers are separated leaving tufts of cotton to mark both pieces.

As a third choice for marking, tailors' chalk or a chalk pencil could be used. This does not give a really crisp, accurate line and it tends to rub off during sewing, but it is a very quick method of marking and will not damage the garment as it brushes off easily. Chalk is useful for marking a large 'W.S.' on fabrics with similar right and wrong sides to avoid confusion, and for drawing arrows on the W.S. of pile fabrics or one-way prints so that all the pieces are cut in the same direction. Lastly, it is invaluable when fitting as alterations may be marked on the R.S. of garments with no fear of damaging it.

TREATMENT OF SPECIAL FABRICS

There are several fabrics which, because of the nature of their make-up, require individual handling to ensure the production of perfect garments.

Stripes

Stripes are woven or printed on either a lengthwise or crosswise grain with an even or an uneven design. As crosswise stripes lie horizontally on a finished garment they are probably best avoided with maternity wear, as no pregnant woman wishes to emphasise her width. Lengthwise stripes, however, would be very flattering as they hang vertically and give a slimmer effect.

The design of an 'even' stripe is identical whether looked at from left to right or right to left, whereas an 'uneven' stripe has an irregular pattern and so looks different in each direction. Cutting out an even stripe is simple as, assuming the fabric does not 'shade', the pattern pieces may be pinned on in an up and down direction known as a 'without-nap' layout. This is usually far more economical than the 'with-nap' layout that must be used on uneven stripes. In this case, every pattern piece must be laid on the fabric in the same direction so that the stripes run evenly around the body of the finished garment.

Stripes must be perfectly matched at C.F. and C.B. and at the sides seams if possible. Use the pattern notches to help matching at the seams by laying corresponding notches on the same stripes. If C.F. or C.B. is cut on the fold, place them on a predominant stripe, and if the garment has a yoke, turn the fabric so the stripes run in a different

62 *Making and cutting a tailors' tack*

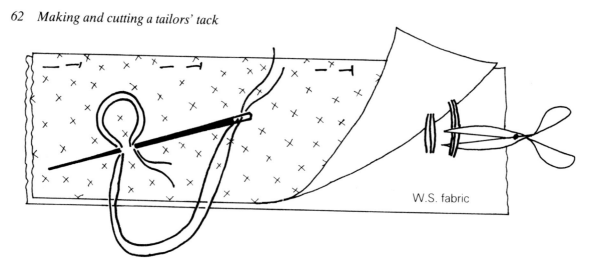

W.S. fabric

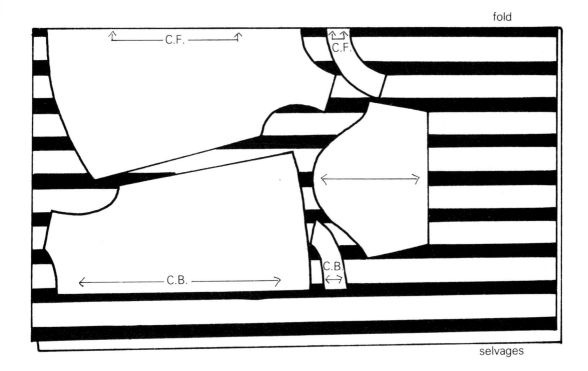

63 *A without-nap layout on even stripes*

64 *A with-nap layout on uneven stripes*

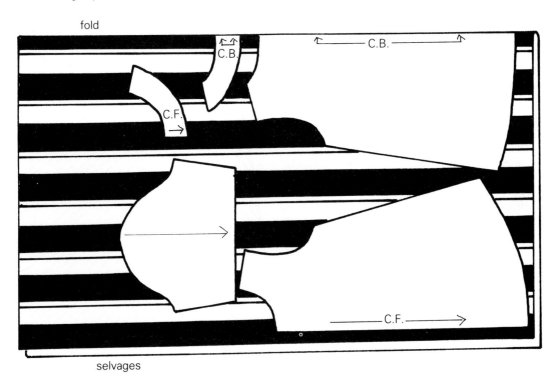

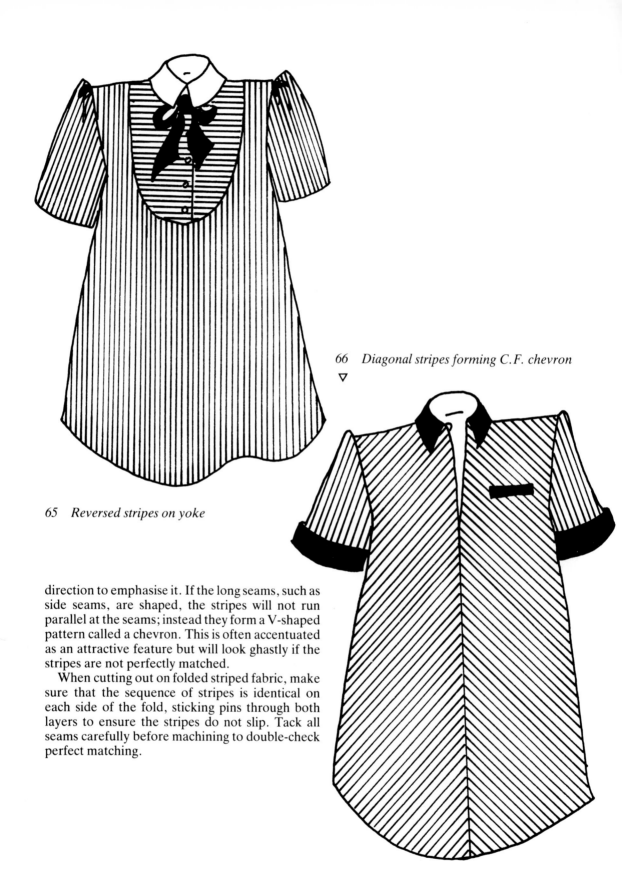

66   *Diagonal stripes forming C.F. chevron*

65   *Reversed stripes on yoke*

direction to emphasise it. If the long seams, such as side seams, are shaped, the stripes will not run parallel at the seams; instead they form a V-shaped pattern called a chevron. This is often accentuated as an attractive feature but will look ghastly if the stripes are not perfectly matched.

When cutting out on folded striped fabric, make sure that the sequence of stripes is identical on each side of the fold, sticking pins through both layers to ensure the stripes do not slip. Tack all seams carefully before machining to double-check perfect matching.

Plaids and checks

These fabrics are made with two sets of stripes crossing over each other at right angles with even or uneven designs. Because plaids and checks must be matched in both directions, the simplest styles with few design lines are usually the most successful. For example, C.F. and C.B. folds eliminate the need to match these seams so you need only concentrate on the shoulder and side seams.

Even checks can be cut out using a without-nap layout, while the uneven ones must be cut using a with-nap layout. Make sure that a predominant

check does not crossover exactly on the bust point, and try to place a predominant vertical stripe down the C.F. and C.B. to balance the garment.

Fold checked fabric to match evenly on either side of the foldline and stick pins through all layers at random to hold them in place. Notches will help to match checks, but do remember that it is the stitching line by the notches which needs to be matched, not the cutting line.

67   Dress made in an uneven plaid

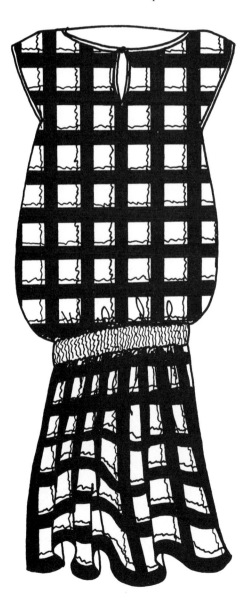

68   An even check

69   An uneven plaid

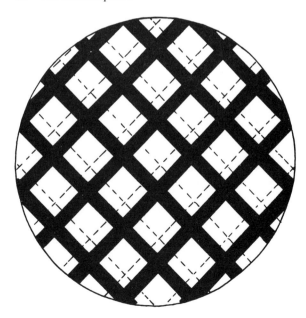

Patterned fabrics

Always examine these carefully before laying on the pattern pieces to see whether or not they have a one-way design. If they do, or you are at all in doubt, use a with-nap layout. When cutting out a very large design, be aware of the positioning of the print on the garment; you would not like to end up with two large cabbage-roses over your bust. It might be helpful, though time-consuming, to cut out pieces from a large printed design on single fabric so you can see exactly where you place your pattern with regard to the fabric design.

70 *Open layout for patterned fabric*

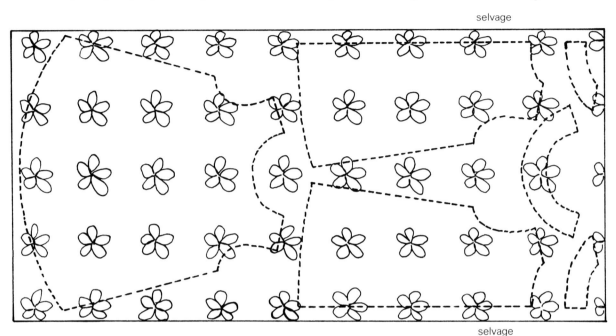

selvage

selvage

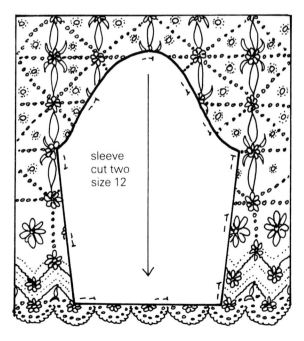

71 *Sleeve hem on fancy edge of all-over lace*

sleeve
cut two
size 12

Lace

Lace is treated like a patterned fabric as it has a repeating motif which often has a one-way design. If it has a decorative edge, try to use it as a feature of your garment, for example at the hem of sleeves or a yoke or pocket.

Jersey fabrics

These need careful handling to make sure they are not stretched during cutting. Smooth these fabrics carefully on the cutting surface and use lots of pins when attaching the pattern. If you are cutting out a synthetic knitted fabric and it is off grain, you will not be able to straighten it; so cut out with an open lay, that is on single fabric, following the lengthwise grain. Cotton jersey fabrics can often be pulled back into shape using the same method as for woven fabrics. Stay stitch the edges of jersey pieces as soon as you remove the pattern to stop them stretching.

Pile fabrics

These are fabrics such as velvet and corduroy which have little 'hairs' on the right side forming the pile. Run your finger up and down these fabrics on the lengthwise grain and you will see that the pile lies smoothly in one direction and not in the other. A deeper colour and more luxurious look, suitable for evening wear, is obtained if the pile lies smoothly upwards towards your face, while in the opposite direction the colour is paler but the garment will be more hard-wearing. A with-nap layout must definitely be used on pile fabrics, and in order to eliminate bulk try to use lining or a matching fine fabric for facing etc.

Shading fabrics

Certain materials such as velvet, corduroy and satin all 'shade', or look dark and light, when held in different directions. Many new fabrics, even unexpected ones, can sometimes have a slight shading difference. If at all in doubt do use a with-nap layout, as pieces cut out in reverse directions, and which shade, will stick out like a sore thumb on a finished garment.

LINING

If you need to line a garment or a section of one, select a lining of the same colour and a suitable weight. Use woven linings with woven fabrics and knitted ones with knitted materials and use washable linings only with washable fabrics.

INTERFACING

Interfacings are put into garments to give strength or crispness or to act as a stay. It is important to think carefully before selecting an interfacing as the wrong choice for the fabric could ruin the garment. There is a wide range of interfacings available: some are woven, knitted or bonded, some washable or dry-clean only. They may be fusible or of the sew-in variety, and come in various weights, colours and fibre contents. As with all linings and trimmings, interfacing must be matched as closely as possible to the fabric for successful results.

Fusible interfacings are easiest to work with as, once they have been fused to the W.S. of fabric with an iron, they are treated as one and cannot slip around while sewing the garment together. Of course, they are not suitable for use on all fabrics so should be tested on a scrap beforehand to ensure the glue does not show through on the R.S. or that it does not make the fabric too rigid and board-like.

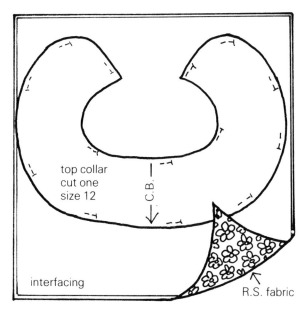

72   *Interfacing fused to fabric before cutting out collar*

When fusing, place the W.S. of the fabric upwards on the ironing board and place the glued side of the interfacing down on top. Press the iron down on a section then lift it off. Do not slide the iron back and forth as the interfacing may slip. Begin with a medium heat and gradually increase the temperature if needed. Some fusibles need steam or a damp press cloth to help them stick.

Non-fusibles, or the sew-in variety, must be carefully pinned then tacked to the W.S. of the cuff, collar or yoke. Great care must be taken to keep both the interfacing and fabric smooth, or there will be a bubbly effect when sewn together.

Like all trimmings, interfacing could shrink when laundered, so, having tested the fabric for shrinkage, it is a wise precaution to test the interfacing. If you find it does shrink, roughly cut out rectangles of fabric for collar, cuffs, facings etc. Fuse the interfacing to the fabric with a damp press cloth then, when it is completely dry and cool, accurately cut out the pieces.

Woven and knitted interfacings must be cut out using exactly the same grain as the garment; bonded ones, however, are more economical as they may be cut in any direction because they have no grain. Often it is appropriate to use different interfacings on different sections of a garment, with a stiff fusible in the collar and cuffs and a softer non-fusible down the C.F. to act as a stay for the buttons and buttonholes.

4. Sewing Methods

Nearly all home dressmakers these days seem to own a sewing machine; no one seems to have the time to sit for endless hours painstakingly sewing entire garments by hand. Modern sewing machines are extremely sophisticated and are able to do several processes which previously could only be worked by hand. Zig-zag stitching, buttonholes, attaching buttons, complicated embroidery, appliqué, darning, hemming and gathering can all speedily be done by machine; but, despite all this, hand sewing still has its place. There is a very peaceful, relaxing quality about sitting with your feet up, perhaps watching the television, and doing bits of hand sewing. This is especially so when you're pregnant and should try and sit quietly when possible.

Some processes are best worked by hand, especially if you lack the confidence of doing it by machine or perhaps your machine is an unsophisticated model. The long seams, such as side seams, are rather boring to sew by hand so perhaps these could be done by machine and then neatened by hand. Always use the methods you find easiest, whether by hand or machine, and that way you will have excellent results.

USING A SEWING MACHINE

Before machining a garment, the stitching should be tested on a scrap of the fabric to see if any adjustment is needed to the tension or stitch size. If the tension seems too tight or too loose, it really is a case of trial and error to adjust it, as sewing machines all vary and therefore need individual adjustment.

If the stitches are too tight, the tension dial should be turned to a looser setting, while loose stitches need the tension to be tightened.

Stitch sizes should be altered for different fabrics, with very fine materials needing 14 or 16 stitches per 2.5cm (1in), medium weights requiring 10 or 12 and heavier fabrics needing 8 or 10 stitches per 2.5cm (1in).

For machine tacking use the longest stitch possible as this will hold the sections firmly together but will be easy to remove afterwards. For gathering use 8 to 12 stitches per 2.5cm (1in) with the longer stitches giving fuller gathers. Remember when gathering to fasten off the stitching at one end and leave long threads at the other so that it will be easy to pull the bobin thread to form the gathers.

Zig-zag machine stitching is a great asset to home dressmakers as it is used as a quick method of neatening S.A.s and also for decorative stitching. If used with a very small stitch size, it is a good stitch for sewing the seams of jersey fabrics as it stretches and therefore prevents the seams from splitting.

HAND STITCHING

Tacking

Tacking is used to secure two or more sections of a garment together before machining. It is especially important for accurately matching stripes or checks and for joining an eased section to a flat section, e.g. inserting a sleeve. Use contrast-coloured tacking cotton and work from right to left, taking even stitches 6mm (¼in) to 2cm (¾in) apart, depending on the thickness of the fabric.

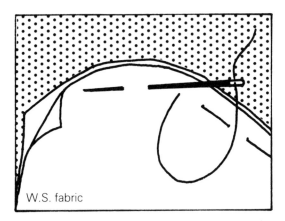

73   Tacking a curved seam

Running stitch

The most basic hand stitch, this is often used for sewing fine tucks, for hand quilting, for gathering or decorative embroidery. It is worked from right to left, taking several even stitches on the needle before pulling it through. The stitch size varies from 2mm (¹⁄₁₆in) for tucks to 6mm (¼in) for gathering.

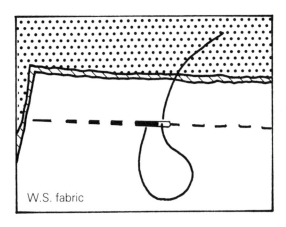

74   Running stitch

Back stitch

This stitch is stronger than running stitch and therefore may be used for seams and areas where a strong hand stitch is required. There are no gaps between the stitches on the upper side, while they overlap on the underside. To make this stitch, go back 3mm (⅛in) on the upper side and then forward 6mm (¼in) on the underside and repeat.

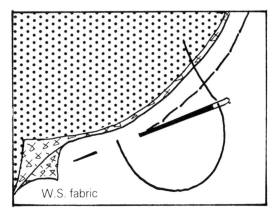

75   Back stitch

Hem stitch

This is a strong method of hand sewing a hem without it showing on the R.S. Having tacked and lightly pressed the hem, use the needle at a slanting angle, taking up one thread from the W.S. of the fabric then several from the folded edge of the hem, and repeat.

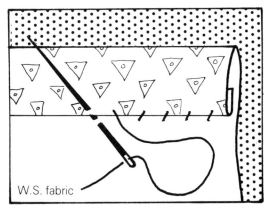

76   Hem stitch

SEAMS

Plain seam

This is the most basic seam used in dressmaking to join two sections of a garment together. Place both R.S.s together, holding them in position with pins inserted at right angles to the seam. Sew along the seam line by machine or with back stitch. Usually, this seam is pressed open and the raw edges suitably neatened, but often, on side or shoulder seams of blouses or very fine fabrics, the S.A.s are pressed together towards the back and neatened together.

When using a plain seam to attach a gathered or pleated section to a yoke, the S.A.s must be pressed together towards the flat yoke and held in place with one or two rows of top stitching.

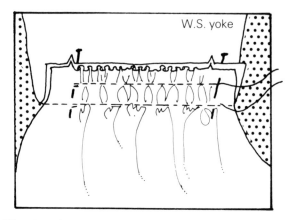

79   *Attaching gathering to a flat yoke*

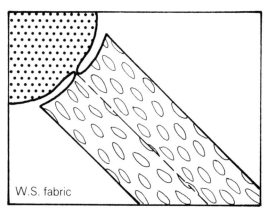

77   *Plain seam pressed open*

Shaped seams

Curved seams such as collars, yoke seams or necklines must be clipped in order to lie flat. A convex or outward curve, e.g. the outer edge of a Peter Pan collar, needs V-shaped notches clipped out of the S.A. 6mm (¼in) apart. This reduces the bulk, giving a smooth curve to the finished collar. A concave or inward curve, e.g. the neckline of a garment, needs only straight snips every 6mm (¼in). When attaching a curved section to a flat one, the stitching lines must be stay-stitched, then the S.A.s clipped or notched, depending on the curve, before joining the two sections. Do remember when sewing curves that it is the length of the stitching line that is important to match, not the cut edge.

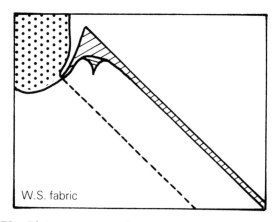

78   *Plain seam pressed to one side*

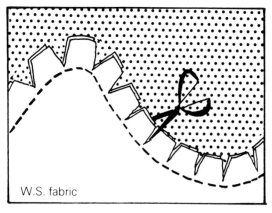

80   *S.A.s notched on an outward curve and clipped on an inward curve*

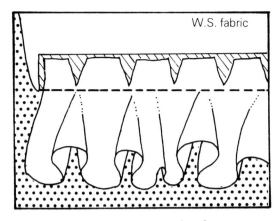

81 Attaching a curve to a straight edge

Layering

Seams to be bagged out, e.g. the outer edges of collars, must be layered to reduce bulk and give a professional finish. This means that the S.A.s of the top collar, the interfacing and the undercollar all need to be trimmed to different widths. This ensures that they do not form an impression of a ridge around the edge of the finished collar.

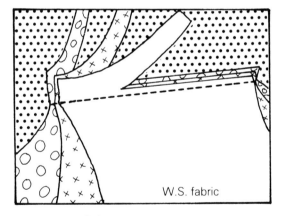

82 Layering S.A.s

French seam

This is a useful seam for sheer fabrics as it gives the neatest possible seam finish. It is also useful if you intend to casually roll up your sleeves or the hems of trousers. Place W.S.s together and stitch 1cm (⅜in) away from the edge, then trim this seam down to 3mm (⅛in) wide. Press this minute seam open, then fold R.S.s together along the first seam line and stitch 6mm (¼in) from the edge, thus enclosing all the raw edges.

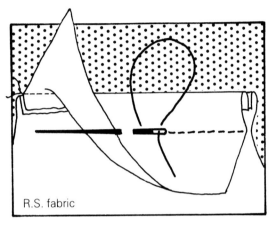

83 A French seam

Fastening off

This must be done correctly and securely at the start and finish of each seam to prevent garments falling apart. The easiest method is to leave long bobbin and needle threads then use them to tie a couple of secure knots. Alternatively, these stitching cottons can be threaded together through a needle and fastened off by making a few back stitches by hand. If you are a confident machinist then the speediest method of fastening off is to sew about three stitches of the seam then reverse the stitching over these three stitches before continuing along the seam.

Seam finishes

A good seam finish not only gives a neat, professional finish to the inside of a garment but also strengthens the seam by ensuring it does not fray.

Pinking

Using pinking shears is the quickest way to neaten a S.A. To strengthen this finish, machine a row of stitching 6mm (¼in) from the cut edge, then evenly cut the edge with pinking shears.

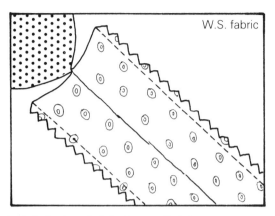

84 *Stitched and pinked seam finish*

Zig-zag stitching

This is a fast efficient machine finish worked close to the raw edge or edges, with a smaller stitch being used on fine fabrics and a larger stitch on heavier, looser woven ones.

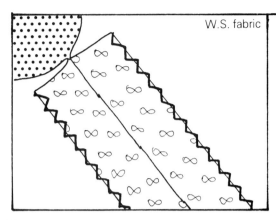

86 *Zig-zag to neaten a seam*

Overcasting

An excellent hand finish for a seam; worked from right to left, small even stitches are taken over the raw edge or edges at a slight angle.

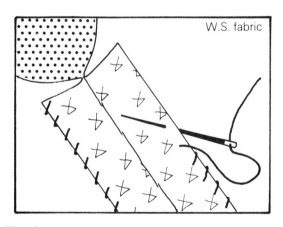

85 *Overcasting to neaten a seam*

Turned and stitched finish

This is a neat finish but may be too bulky for use on heavy fabrics. The cut edge is turned over 6mm (¼in) then stitched 3mm (⅛in) from the fold.

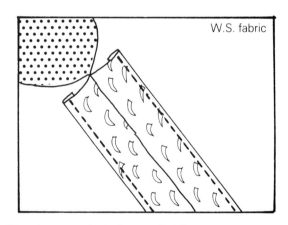

87 *A turn and stitch seam finish*

HEMS

Machined hem

This type of hem is extremely quick to sew and used on hems of blouses, trousers, nightwear, and sometimes even on dresses and skirts. Allow 2cm (¾in) for this hem. Turn up 6mm (¼in) and stitch in place near the foldline, then turn up another 13mm (½in) and stitch in place over the first row of stitching.

DARTS

Fold the dart along its foldline and insert pins at right angles to the fold. Tack along stitching line then machine or back stitch the dart, starting at the wider end. At the point of the dart, make two or three stitches directly along the foldline. This is extremely important to eliminate a bubble effect at the point of the dart. Fasten off at both ends securely.

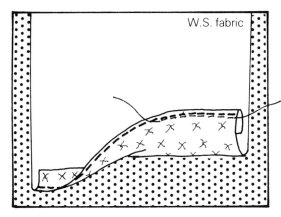

88   A machined hem

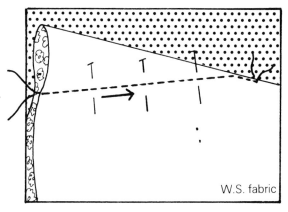

90   Stitching a dart

Pin hem

A very small, dainty hem used on sheer fabrics and the edges of frills. Allow 1cm (⅜in) for this hem. Turn up 6mm (¼in) and machine this in place as close as possible to the fold. Use a sharp pair of small scissors to trim away close to the row of stitching. Fold this minute hem over another 3mm (⅛in) and stitch in place over the previous row of stitching.

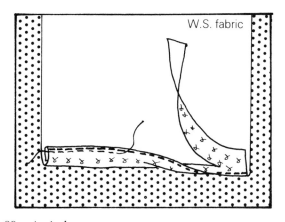

89   A pin hem

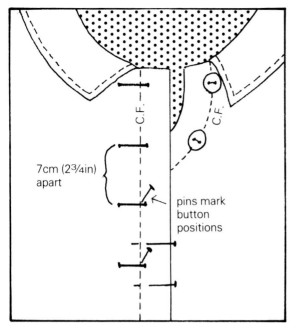

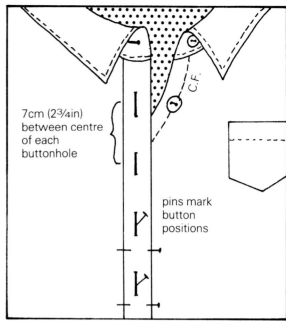

91 *Horizontal button positioning*   92 *Vertical button positioning*

BUTTONS AND BUTTONHOLES

When positioning buttons and buttonholes on maternity garments, place them quite close together with about 7cm (2¾in) between the centre of each button; on a C.F. opening always position a button exactly at bust level to avoid an embarrassing gaping front.

Buttonholes must be made through at least three layers – the outer section, the interfacing and the facing – to ensure strength, and they may be made by hand or machine. Practice making a buttonhole on a scrap of the fabric and interfacing before making them on the finished garment; they are the last process in making a garment and it would be a shame to ruin it with poor buttonholes.

TOP STITCHING

This is stitching made on the outside of a garment to give it a neat professional finish. It may be used purely for decorative purposes or, for example, around the edges of yokes, collars and cuffs to hold all the layers together. Position the outer edge of the machine foot along the outer edge of the collar or cuff, and follow this edge as a guide to ensure a straight row of top stitching which is perfectly parallel to the edge. Contrast-coloured cotton or shiny buttonhole twist can be used to make a special feature of the top stitching.

ELASTICATED WAISTS

Adjustable, elasticated waistlines are the most comfortable for maternity skirts, trousers or shorts. Make a folded channel at the waist leaving a small gap in the seam at one side. Thread special buttonhole elastic through the channel, securing one end by the gap and leaving the other hanging like a long tail inside the garment. Sew a small button inside the waist and use this to secure the elastic at whatever tension feels comfortable as the waist expands.

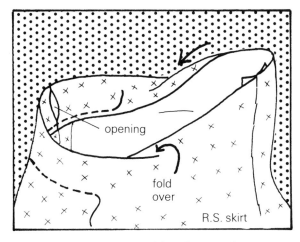

93 Folded waist channel for elasticated waist

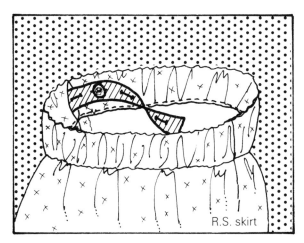

94 Buttonhole elastic threaded through channel and secured with a button

EASY TIPS

Several products are now available on the market which make home dressmaking much quicker and easier and give excellent results.

Hems need no longer be felled by hand, as there is now a narrow fusible web with 'glue' on both sides which does the job. When placed between the hem and the garment and ironed through a damp press cloth, the heat gently melts the glue and the hem is held securely and permanently in place.

A similar fusible web can be used for holding appliqué sections in position – a great help when sewing around the edges.

To eliminate the tacking of seams, zips, patch pockets and for matching stripes, there is now a 'glue' stick to do it for you. It looks like a lipstick and, when rubbed gently over the surface of the fabric, makes it sticky so that two sections of fabric can easily be 'stuck' together in position for stitching.

Similarly, there is a double-sided sticky tape available to eliminate tacking. When placed between two sections of fabric and the adhesive backing peeled away, both sections will be held together securely for stitching.

If buttons and buttonholes are a bit of a problem, Velcro now make stick-on and sew spots which make a very good non-bulky fastening. These dots stick easily in position and so do not slip around while being sewn on. Buttons could be quickly sewn on over these spots for decorative purposes.

Another alternative fastening which looks very attractive is studs hammered onto the garment. These come with a wide range of multi-coloured heads and are quick to attach with the use of a hammer.

PRESSING

Garments should be ironed after each seam and section is stitched to ensure a smooth and accurate assembly with excellent, professional-looking results. Keep the iron and ironing board set out near your sewing machine with both a dry and a damp press cloth close at hand.

Before cutting out, both the pattern and the fabric must be pressed. The pattern needs to be smoothed out using a dry iron, while the fabric should be pressed with steam or through a damp press cloth. Unless it is vital to press fabric or a section of a garment on the R.S. then always iron on the W.S. in case the iron marks the fabric with a 'shine'. Begin pressing always using a low temperature setting and gradually increasing it if necessary for the fabric.

Ironing should be carried out as an up and down action, not a back and forth sliding movement as this may stretch and distort the fabric.

Do keep the underside of the iron clean; there are several good iron cleaning products available and without them a dirty iron can leave awful marks on a garment.

Pressing fabrics

Cottons and linens are pressed using high temperatures and steam or a damp press cloth to remove creases. Always let the fabric cool down and dry before handling it otherwise you will put back more creases than you started with. These fabrics must be sewn using compatible threads; for example, if nylon thread is used to sew cotton fabric, it will melt under the high pressing temperatures and the garment will fall apart.

Silk fabrics require a medium temperature setting for pressing and minimum steam through a dry press cloth as they tend to watermark easily.

Polyesters, nylons, rayons and other synthetic fabrics should be pressed with quite a low temperature setting as they can melt if subjected to high temperatures.

Lace fabrics are pressed at temperatures to suit the fibres of which they are made. If mixed fibres have been used, such as cotton and polyester, a cool temperature setting is needed, while pure cotton lace needs more heat. Do press lace through a press cloth to prevent the point of the iron tearing it.

Pile fabrics such as velvet or corduroy are pressed most successfully on the W.S. over a needle-board. This prevents the pile from being flattened. Without the use of a needleboard, stand the iron on its heel and draw the W.S. of the fabric across the iron. A third method is to hang the garment made of pile fabric in a steamy bathroom. The steam will remove the creases but it must be thoroughly dried before it is handled or worn.

Pressing the garment

Seams Seams should be pressed on the W.S as they are sewn. First they are pressed closed along the row of stitching then pressed open using the point of the iron. Do not lay the iron flat on a seam as you press it open as this will form seam impressions through on the R.S. If the S.A.s are to be pressed together to one side, such as a yoke seam, press the seam open then together to one side to ensure a smooth seamline.

Collars Collars must be pressed as carefully as they are sewn for perfect results. Top press them through a cloth to prevent the points and seams from shining, and press the outer seams so that they roll 2mm (1/16in) to the underside and so are hidden. When a collar has a nice roll to it, do not press it flat on the board but retain the roll by pressing it over the curved edge of the ironing board.

Sleeves The armhole seam should be pressed as soon as the sleeves are attached. Lay the seam on the ironing board with the W.S. of the sleeve uppermost and press the seam with the point of the iron from the cut edges to the stitching line, slowly working around the armhole. The underarm S.A.s of the armhole should stand upwards while the sleeve head section is very gently pressed to lie towards the sleeve.

When top pressing a sleeve it should not be pressed flat on the board, as that will form a crease running from shoulder to hem. Either use a narrow sleeve board or press at the edge of the ironing board, folding the sleeve over and over so that it may all be ironed but without introducing a crease.

Hems These must be ironed very gently just to form a crease along the foldline, using the point of the iron. Do not lay the iron flat over the hem as this will form an unsightly hem impression on the right side.

Gathering Press gathers with the point of the iron moving gently upwards in between the gathers. Never place an iron flat on top of gathering as this will squash and crease it, loosing the soft effect.

Darts Darts are pressed in a similar way to seams, first being pressed flat along the stitching line then pressed open or to one side. Use the point

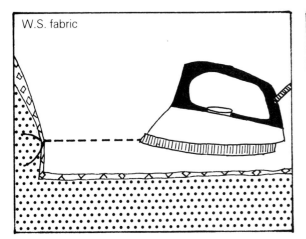

W.S. fabric

95 *Seam firstly pressed along row of stitching*

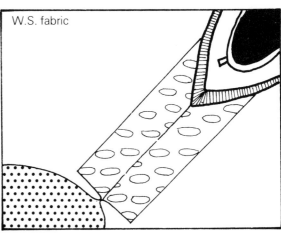

W.S. fabric

96 *Seam secondly pressed open with toe of iron*

of the iron and always begin pressing at the wide end of the dart, slowly moving along to the point of the dart. Place thick, brown paper between the dart and the garment to avoid an impression on the R.S. Horizontal darts running from shoulder to bust line are pressed toward the centre, while underarm darts are pressed downwards.

Top pressing   A finished garment always needs a good top press before it is ready to wear. If the underpressing has been conscientiously done at each stage, then the top pressing will only be necessary to smooth out wrinkles and small creases caused through handling.

5. Decorative Touches

Very simple maternity shapes are often the most flattering and successful, and if one finds a perfect shape it is tempting to make several garments from the same pattern. This is a good idea, but to ring the changes there are a variety of decorative touches which could be added to each garment giving them their own individual look.

A basic smock shape could be made, first with circular frills attached around the neck and by the cuffs. The next version could have an appliqué design applied to the yoke making it look like multi-coloured patchwork. A third smock could be made for the evening in a luxurious dark velvet with a creamy satin embroidered collar and pretty pearl buttons down the front. For a cheerful daytime dress the basic smock could be made again in bright cotton poplin with alternate rows of contrasting ric-rac and decorative braid across the yoke and patch pockets. All four garments would have a very individual look and no one would possibly guess they were all made from the same pattern.

By making your own maternity clothes, you can afford to spend a bit extra on the trimmings. These are well worth the cost as they make the difference between a rather ordinary-looking garment and one with a distinctively expensive look.

FRILLS

These give a soft, feminine look to maternity clothes. They may be made either as straight-cut frills or circular ones.

Straight-cut frills

These are made, as the name suggests, as long straight strips of fabric 1½ to 3 times the finished length, depending on how full you want the gathers to be. They must always be cut out across the width of the fabric in order to gather nicely, even though this involves several joins on long frills. If they are cut out on the opposite grain, because of the stronger lengthwise threads, the frills will form hard, irregular ridges instead of soft gathers. The only occasion on which this rule should be broken is when using a striped fabric and the stripes are required to run a certain way on the frills as a design feature.

Straight frills are gathered using two rows of stitching, one on the finished seamline and the other 6mm (¼in) away towards the cut edge. Use the largest stitch on the sewing machine and fasten

97 *Straight frills always cut across the fabric*

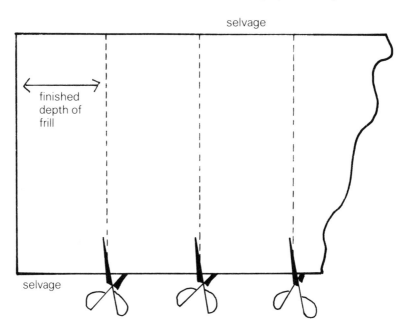

selvage

finished depth of frill

selvage

off the stitching securely at one end before pulling the bobbin threads to form the gathers. When these are the required fullness, secure the threads around a pin and adjust the gathers evenly. When making very long frills, divide the frill and the garment section to which it is to be attached into halves or quarters. Pin these sections together before pulling the gathering threads, as it is always easier, and more accurate, to work on a smaller section.

When machining a frill onto a garment always work with the gathered section uppermost as it is easier to guide the machine accurately along the line of gathering.

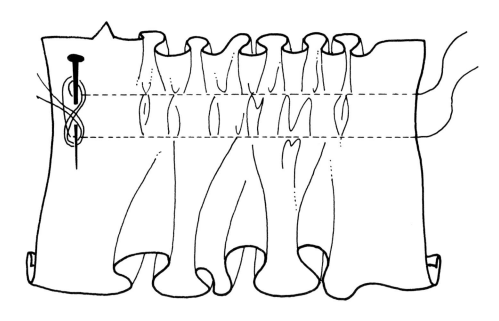

△
98   *Two rows of gathering secured around a pin*   99   *Long frills pinned to garment in sections*
▽

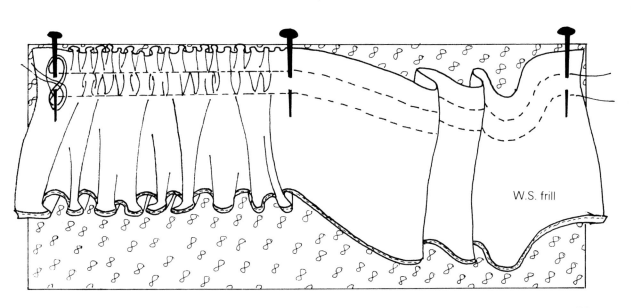

W.S. frill

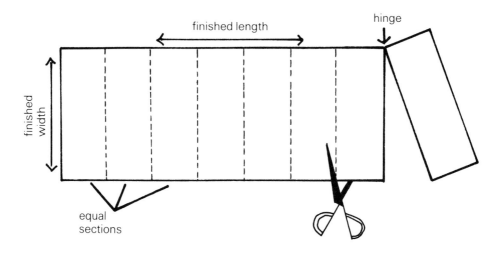

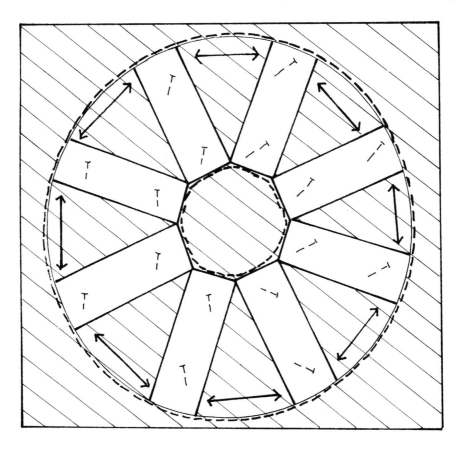

Circular-cut frills

These are cut as circles, frilling only at the outer edge. The smaller the inner circle is made, the fuller the frills will be.

To construct a pattern for these frills, draw a rectangle the finished length of the pattern by the required width. Cut this rectangle at regular intervals leaving tiny 'hinges' along one edge. Carefully spread the cut rectangle until it forms a circle, then add S.A.s. If a very long full frill is required then several circles must be made and joined together with a seam, such as a French seam, which is neat on both sides.

Neatening frill edges

Several methods can be used to neaten the edges of frills depending on the type of fabric, type of frill or width of frill being used.

A very wide straight frill, e.g. at the hem of a dress, may be given a hand felled hem, but usually a machined hem is used on frills to save time. Very narrow straight frills are often pin hemmed or decoratively hemmed using a zig-zag stitch. Decide on the hem finish you wish to use before cutting out the frills so that you can add the appropriate S.A.s.

Circular frills are most often given a dainty machined pin hem, but a narrow lace edging could be zig-zagged on as an alternative.

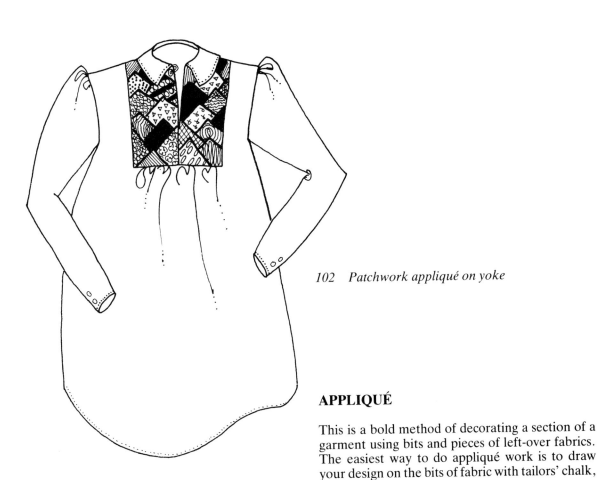

102 Patchwork appliqué on yoke

APPLIQUÉ

This is a bold method of decorating a section of a garment using bits and pieces of left-over fabrics. The easiest way to do appliqué work is to draw your design on the bits of fabric with tailors' chalk, then cut them out and iron them onto the garment using the special fusible web now available. There is no need to sew these appliqué pieces to the garment, though they often look attractive if the edges are emphasised with a zig-zag or embroidery stitch.

BRAID

There is a huge variety of braid available; it comes in all sorts of colours, widths, designs and textures. A few rows of mix 'n' match braid across a yoke, on patch pockets or around the hem of a tiered dress is a very quick and effective way to decorate a garment. Decide on the positioning of the braid and then mark guidelines on the garment with tailors' chalk. Flat braids and ric-rac braids should be tacked in place then machined on with a straight stitch or hem-stitched by hand along each edge.

Folded braid can be used to neaten as well as decorate the raw edges around a collar, pair of cuffs or patch pockets. This is a special braid which is bought ready-folded; it is constructed on the bias grain and so is equally successful whether being used on straight edges or around curves. It comes folded just off-centre and should be tacked in place over the raw edges with the narrower section on the R.S. of the garment. When stitched on through all thicknesses, the stitches will always secure the wider under section. Remember to gently stretch the outer, folded edge when applying this braid to an outer curve, and to stretch the inner, open edges when neatening an inner curve.

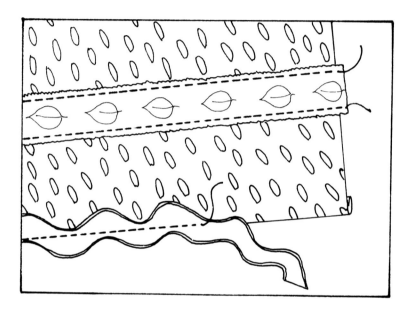

103   Flat braid stitching in place and ric-rac used as an edging

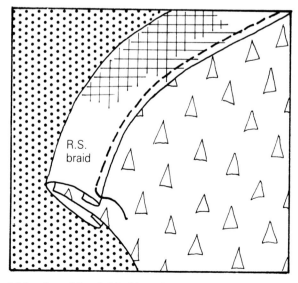

104   Attaching folded bias braid

82

LACE

Despite the vast selection there are basically only three types of lace available: insertion lace, edging lace and all-over lace. When selecting lace for a garment, apart from choosing the correct width, colour and design, do get one of compatible fibre content; for example, cotton lace edging on a polyester smock would be totally unsuitable as it would need high temperatures to iron it which would severely burn the polyester fabric. Also, it is well worth dipping lace in a bowl of warm water then letting it dry fully before using it, just in case it shrinks.

Insertion lace

This type of lace has two finished edges, either straight or scalloped, and is inserted, as the name suggests, between two sections of a garment. A zig-zag stitch makes lace insertion an easy process. Tack the lace in position then zig-zag along both edges. Use a sharp pair of scissors and cut away the fabric under the lace close to the stitching. Alternatively, without a zig-zag stitch, a row of straight machine stitching must be made along each edge. When the fabric under the lace is trimmed away, a small amount should be left so that it may be overcast by hand to prevent the raw edges fraying.

This type of lace looks attractive inserted in several areas of a garment. It can be used very successfully in maternity wear to make a feature of sleeves, with a couple of rows being inserted down the length of the sleeve or diagonally through the sleeve. Several rows can be inserted in a yoke, perhaps with rows of narrow satin ribbon or braid stitched on between them, or a wider, heavier lace could be inserted just above the hem of a dress.

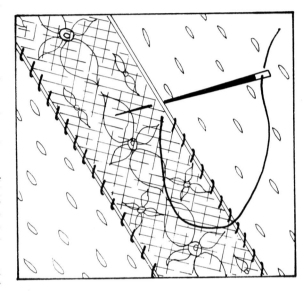

106 *Insertion lace attached by hand*

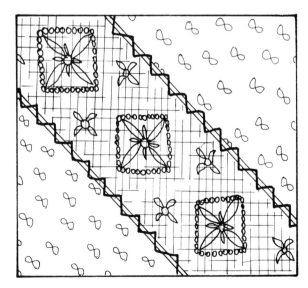

105 *Insertion lace attached with zig-zag*

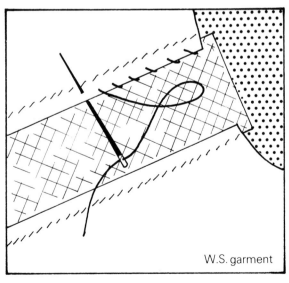

107 *Insertion lace being neatened on the W.S.*

83

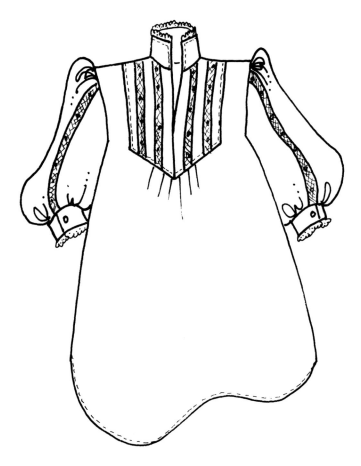

△
*108   Maternity top with edging lace and insertion
lace*

109   Edging lace attached with zig-zag stitch

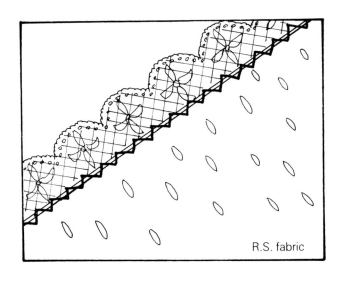

R.S. fabric

Edging lace

This lace has one straight edge and one decorative edge and is used either flat or slightly gathered when attached to an edge of a garment. It is used to edge collars, cuffs, frills, yokes, pockets or hemlines. For a gathered edging, a strong thread is often found in the straight edge and this can be gently pulled to the required length of gathers. Without this strong thread, a row of gathering stitches must be made by hand or machine near the straight edge. The lace is tacked in position then attached with a zig-zag stitch or hand sewn with a row of close whip-stitching.

All-over lace

This is used when large areas of lace are required such as for yokes, sleeves, cuffs or for an entire lace evening jacket. It is made like a printed fabric, being the same width with a repeating motif, and is bought by the metre. Look carefully at the pattern of the lace when placing the paper pattern on it as it could be a one-way design. Select an attractive motif for a C.F. feature and, if cutting out a pair of left and right yokes, do place similar motifs in the centre of each yoke.

110   All-over lace jacket

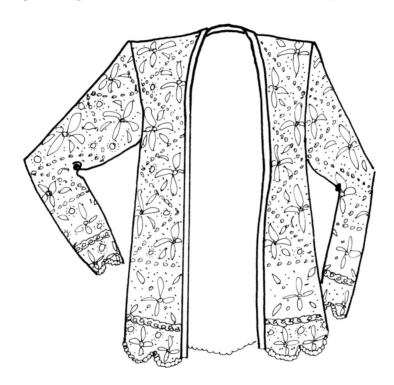

EMBROIDERY

This may be worked by hand or machine and is a bright attractive method of decoration. A spray of flowers would brighten up the yoke of a smock or a pair of patch pockets. Embroidery stitches could be used with appliqué or a small section of quilting and an embroidered monogram would add a very expensive touch to the breast pocket of an over-blouse.

TUCKS

These are a widely-used feature on maternity clothes as not only do they look smart but they are also a good method of introducing fullness over the tummy.

Tucks are folds of fabric stitched in position on the R.S. of garments and are usually made in groups for a decorative effect. If an entire section of a garment is to be tucked, e.g. on a yoke, it is advisable to make all the tucks on a section of fabric before cutting out the yoke, because no matter how carefully tucks are measured and sewn, the smallest discrepancy on each tuck would leave a yoke entirely the wrong size and shape for the garment. By placing the yoke pattern on a ready-tucked piece of fabric, a perfect yoke can be guaranteed.

When marking tucks it is vital to begin exactly on the straight grain to ensure the tucks lie flat; the most accurate way to find this grain is to pull a single thread from the fabric on the foldline of the first tuck. After pressing this foldline, measure the required width of tuck with a tape measure or gauge. Tack, stitch, press it flat then measure the next tuck.

When making several pin tucks on very fine fabric, it might be easiest to pull a thread on the fold of each tuck because, as the name suggest, they are stitched only a pin's width away from the fold. Pin tucks are not pressed flat like wider tucks but they are left to stand up on their own.

On the front of maternity tops or dresses, groups of tucks are often stitched from the shoulders and neckline down to about bust level then released, adding extra fullness over the tummy. Do fasten off the stitching securely at the bottom of these tucks to ensure they do not come apart.

111   Top with embroidery on tucks

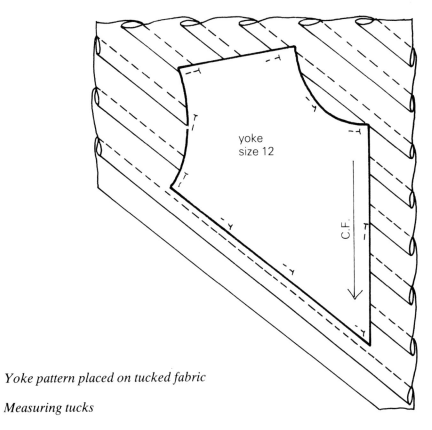

yoke
size 12

C.F.

112 *Yoke pattern placed on tucked fabric*

113 *Measuring tucks*

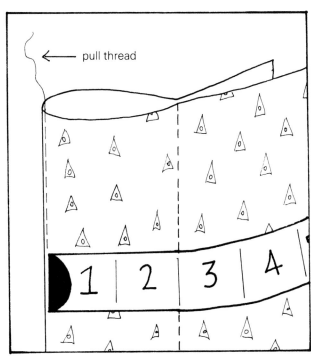

← pull thread

1 | 2 | 3 | 4 |

QUILTING

Small sections of quilting can make an unusual feature of a yoke or pair of cuffs on a maternity outfit. The easiest method of quilting a small area is to make a template on thin paper, drawing on the stitching lines of the design. Place the paper template on top of a piece of the fabric then place both of these on a layer of wadding then onto a backing fabric. Use several pins to hold all four layers securely together and prevent them from slipping. Stitch by machine or by hand with a small running stitch through all the layers following the design lines of the template. Having completed the stitching, carefully tear away the paper template leaving a perfect, quilted design. Place the yoke or cuff pattern on top of the quilting then cut around it and it will be ready to be attached to the garment.

Do remember that the finished section of quilting will be smaller than the original piece of fabric, so always allow for this contraction.

114   Quilting using a paper template

CONTRAST PIPING

This is inserted in seams such as collar seams, side seams, yokes, shoulders, armholes or pockets to define them and to add interest and smartness to a plain garment. Piping may be bought ready-made or can be produced by covering narrow cord with strips of narrow, bias-cut fabric. When making piping, choose a cord and a fabric with compatible fibres to those of the garment, e.g. cotton cord goes with cotton fabric and a synthetic cord with man-made fabrics. Cut bias strips of fabric about 5cm (2in) wide and fold in half along its length. Place the cord in the fold and tack, then machine using a piping foot, as close to the cord as possible. Trim away the excess S.A.s of the piping so that it is the same width as those of the garment. Sandwich the piping between the R.S.s of the seam with all four raw edges exactly on top of each other. Tack, then machine through all layers as close as possible to the cord. When piping a shaped seam do snip notches in the S.A. of the piping to allow it to lie flat around the curves.

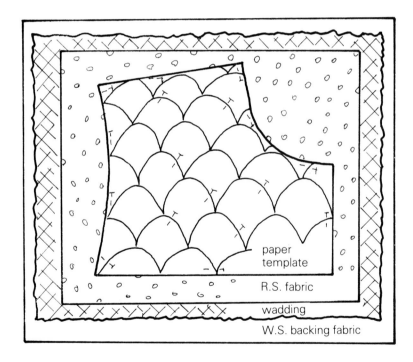

paper
template

R.S. fabric

wadding

W.S. backing fabric

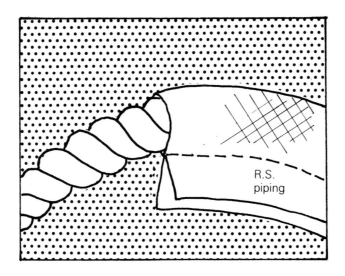

115 *Cord inserted in bias strip to make piping*   116 *Inserting piping*

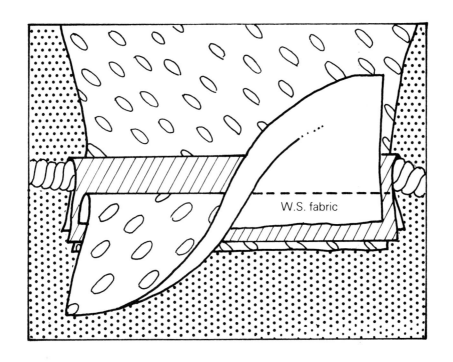

117　*Attaching piping to a curved seam*

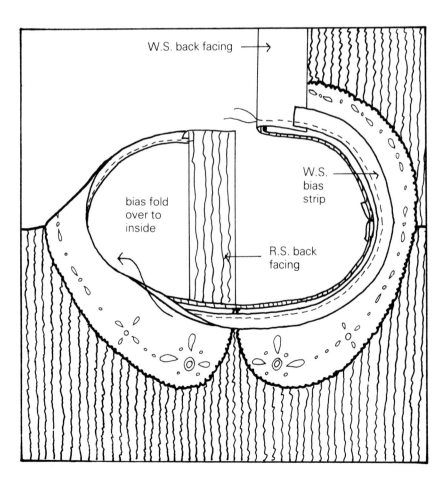

W.S. back facing →

W.S. bias strip →

bias fold over to inside

R.S. back facing

119   Back buttoning for a decorative effect

CONTRAST COLLARS

An easy way to brighten up a plain smock is to attach a contrast collar. The simplest method of doing this is to buy a ready-made one with an attractive embroidered edge. Lay the collar in position on the neckline of the garment then lay a length of bias binding on top. Tack then stitch through all the layers, then fold the bias binding over on to the inside of the neckline and neatly sew it in place with a row of hem stitching.

In addition to these decorative ideas there are several other methods of brightening up and giving an individual look to maternity garments. Buttons are a simple and cheap way of decorating, looking very smart if used close together across a shoulder or yoke or down the C.B. of a skirt or top. Several rows of top stitching using silky buttonhole twist is always smart on collars, cuffs, pockets and yokes as is contrast top stitching. Iron-on motifs of flowers, bows, animals or monograms make quick decoration, as do ribbons, large pussy-cat bows and punched eyelets for lacing.

Designers are always producing new gimmicky ideas for decoration, so if you keep your eyes open when passing shop windows or reading glossy magazines you may suddenly spot the perfect idea for decorating your next outfit.

118   Attaching a ready-made collar

Glossary

Appliqué
A decorative trimming made by attaching small pieces of fabric, forming a design, with zig-zag or slip stitch.

Bag out
The process of neatening the edges of two sections, such as collars, cuffs and neck ties, which must be perfectly neat on both sides with S.A.s hidden between them.

Balance marks
See **notches**.

Bias grain
This lies at a 45 degree angle to the selvage and has quite a lot of 'stretch', so is useful for bindings and facings applied to curved edges.

Binding
A bias strip of fabric used to neaten or trim raw edges.

Blouson
When elastic is threaded through a channel at the hem of a blouse giving a soft, pouched effect.

Body measurements
Exact measurements of bust, waist, hips etc. used to determine size of pattern required.

Button wrap
An extension added to each side of an opening. They overlap to enable the buttons and buttonholes to be fastened.

Chevron
When stripes meet at a seam to form a V-shape.

Clip
Short scissor snips made in the S.A.s of curved seams or corners.

Crosswise grain
Also known as a weft grain, it runs across the width of the fabric.

Dart
A stitched fold of fabric tapering to a point at one or both ends used to give shape to a garment.

Ease
(1) Subtle shaping introduced by joining two seams of different lengths without forming gathers or tucks (e.g. sleeve heads). (2) Extra amounts added to garment to allow for movement by wearer.

Even plaid
The repeat of the colour and design of the plaid is identical in both directions, enabling a without-nap layout to be used.

Even stripe
The repeat of the width and colour of the stripe is identical in both directions.

Facings
Shaped pieces of fabric, usually interfaced, used to neaten necklines, sleeveless armholes, front openings, etc.

Gathering
Fullness introduced to a garment by pulling up two rows of either running stitches or large machine stitches.

Gauge
A simple piece of equipment used for measuring the widths of hems, S.A.s, tucks etc.

Grain
The direction in which the yarns run in fabric. The warp or lengthwise grain lies parallel to the selvage, the weft or crosswise grain lies across the fabric, and the bias grain lies at a 45 degree angle to the selvage. Unless otherwise stated, the grain lines on patterns always follow the lengthwise grain.

Grown-on
A term used when facings, collars or cuffs are cut out all in one piece with the rest of the garment so they are folded, instead of being stitched into place.

Interfacing
Special woven, bonded or knitted fabrics which are either sewn or ironed-on to sections of a garment to stiffen, give body or just act as a stay.

Layout
The positioning of pattern pieces on a length of fabric prior to cutting out.

Lengthwise grain
Also known as selvage grain. It runs down the length of the fabric.

Markings
All the information on a pattern, most of which must be transferred to the fabric pieces after they have been cut out.

Notches
Also known as balance marks. These are small triangles jutting out from the S.A. which help to assemble garments correctly.

Pin tuck
Extremely fine fold of fabric stitched a pin's width from the fold, usually made in groups for decoration.

Pivot
To swivel your work with the machine needle down through the garment to ensure a neat corner (e.g. corners of collars and cuffs).

Pressing cloth   A muslin cloth placed over the fabric or garment when ironing to prevent the iron giving a shine to the fabric. It may be used damp or dry.

Rouleau   Long, narrow fabric 'tubes' with S.A.s enclosed, made from bias strips and cut to short lenghts to make button loops.

S.A.   (seam allowance). An extension of 1.5cm (⅝in) added to the edge of patterns to enable the garment to be sewn together.

Selvage   The strong, finished edge found along both sides of a length of fabric.

Stay stitch   A stabilising row of stitching made just inside the S.A. to prevent the stretching of bias or shaped sections of a garment before it is sewn together.

'Step'   This is formed when a section of the neck edge is bagged out to allow a collar to sit edge to edge or to give space to make a bow with a tie-neck style.

Tacking   Small, even, hand stitches or large machine stitches used to hold two or more sections of a garment securely together for fitting purposes or for machining.

Tailors' tacks   Thread loops made to transfer markings from the pattern to the cut out fabric pieces.

Toile   A mock garment made in calico or an old sheet for fitting purposes.

Top stitching   A row of stitching made on the outside of a garment close to a seam securing the S.A.s to the outer section, or made just for decorative purposes.

Under stitching   A row of machining made close to the stitching line on the underside of collars, cuffs and facings to secure the trimmed S.A.s and thereby prevent the seam rolling over on to the R.S.

Uneven plaid   The repeat of the colour and design of the plaid runs only in one direction so a with-nap layout must be used.

Uneven stripe   The repeat of the width and colour and design of the stripe runs only in one direction so a with-nap layout must be used.

Warp   The lengthwise grain of fabric following the line of the warp threads.

Weft   The crosswise grain of fabric following the line of the weft threads.

With-nap   A term used to indicate that all the pattern pieces must be laid on the fabric in the same direction to achieve a successful finished garment, because the fabric may be a one-way print, a pile fabric or an uneven stripe or plaid.

Without-nap   A term used to indicate that the pattern pieces may be laid on the fabric in an up and down direction without harming the appearance of the finished garment. This applies to plain fabrics, up and down prints and even stripes and plaids.

List of Suppliers

Department stores – dress fabrics and haberdashery

John Lewis Partnership
Oxford Street
London W1 (and branches)

Harrods
Knightsbridge
London SW1

Liberty & Co. Ltd
Regent Street
London W1

Selfridges
Oxford Street
London W1

Dress fabrics

Laura Ashley
71 Lower Sloane Street
London SW1 (and branches)

The Fabric Studio
10 Frith Street
London W1

H. Wolfin and Son
64 Great Titchfield Street
London W1

Strawberry Fayre
Chagford
Newton Abbot
Devon. TQ13 8EN

Whaley's (Bradford) Ltd
Ham's Court
Great Horton
Bradford
West Yorkshire BD7 4EQ

Netta (Liskeard) ltd
15 & 25 Fore Street
Liskeard
Cornwall

George Weil and Sons Ltd
63-65 Riding House Street
London W1

Sewing machines and attachments

Elna Sewing Machines (GB) Ltd
180-182 Tottenham Court Road
London W1P 9LE

Singer Sewing Co. (UK) Ltd
255 High Street
Guildford
Surrey

Bernina Sewing Centre
10 Wardour Street
London W1

Supreme Sewing Machines
189 Streatham High Road
London SW16

Bedford Sewing and Knitting
Machines Ltd
13 Lime Street
Bedford

Frister & Rossmann Sewing
Machines Ltd
Mark Way
Swanley
Kent

Threads and haberdashery

Needle Needs
20 Beauchamp Place
Knightsbridge
London SW1

Tootal Sewing Products
56 Oxford Street
Manchester M60 1HJ

Perivale-Gutermann Ltd
Wadsworth Road
Perivale
Greenford
Middlesex

McCulloch & Wallis Ltd
25-26 New Bond Street
London W1

J. & P. Coats (UK) Ltd
Harlequin Avenue
Great West Road
Brentford
Middlesex

The Cheap Shop
Church Road
Tiptree
Essex

Franklins
13a-15 St Bartolphs St.
Colchester
Essex

Buttons, belts and buckles

Ackerman Buttons Ltd
326 Hackney Road
London E2

Button Queen
19 Marylebone Lane
London W1

Button Box
44 Bedford Street
Covent Garden
London WC2

Harlequin
Lawling House
Stutton
Ipswich
Suffolk

Sewing aids and interfacings

Value House
12 Union Road
Croydon
Surrey

The Vilene Organisation
P.O. Box 3
Greetland
Halifax
Yorkshire

Index